iPhone® 5

FOR

DUMMIES®

PORTABLE EDITION

by Edward C. Baig
USA TODAY Personal Tech columnist
and
Bob LeVitus
Houston Chronicle "Dr. Mac" columnist

WILEY

John Wiley & Sons, Inc.

iPhone® 5 For Dummies®, Portable Edition

Published by
John Wiley & Sons, Inc.
111 River Street
Hoboken, NJ 07030-5774

www.wiley.com

Copyright © 2013 by John Wiley & Sons, Inc., Hoboken, New Jersey

Published by John Wiley & Sons, Inc., Hoboken, New Jersey

Published simultaneously in Canada

For general information on our other products and services, please contact our Customer Care Department within the U.S. at 877-762-2974, outside the U.S. at 317-572-3993, or fax 317-572-4002.

For technical support, please visit www.wiley.com/techsupport.

Wiley publishes in a variety of print and electronic formats and by print-on-demand. Some material included with standard print versions of this book may not be included in e-books or in print-on-demand. If this book refers to media such as a CD or DVD that is not included in the version you purchased, you may download this material at http://booksupport.wiley.com. For more information about Wiley products, visit www.wiley.com.

Library of Congress Control Number: 2012951519

ISBN 978-1-118-50372-0 (pbk); ISBN 978-1-118-55274-2 (ebk); ISBN 978-1-118-55275-9 (ebk); ISBN 978-1-118-55276-6 (ebk)

Manufactured in the United States of America

10 9 8 7 6 5 4 3 2 1

WILEY

Table of Contents

Chapter 9: Getting to Know iPhone Apps 153

Chapter 10: When Good iPhones Go Bad 159

Chapter 11: Ten (Or So) iPhone Tips 171

Index 179

Introduction

*A*s with most products coming out of Apple, the iPhone 5 is beautifully designed and intuitive to use. And although our editors may not want us to reveal this dirty little secret, the truth is that you'll get pretty far just by exploring the iPhone's many functions and features on your own.

But this book is chock-full of solid information and good advice for getting started with your iPhone. We try to give you a thorough tour of the phone and show you how to sync your data, make calls, control your iPhone with your voice, send text messages, surf the Internet, send e-mail, take pictures, play music, watch videos, and download iPhone apps from the App Store. We hope you have a great time getting familiar with your iPhone.

Icons Used in This Book

Little icons appear in the left margins throughout this book. Consider these icons miniature road signs, telling you something extra about the topic at hand or hammering a point home. Here's what the four icons indicate:

These are the juicy morsels and shortcuts that can make the task at hand faster or easier.

This icon emphasizes the stuff we think you ought to retain. You may even jot down a note to yourself in the iPhone.

Put on your propeller beanie hat and pocket protector — this text includes the truly geeky stuff. You can safely ignore this material, but we include it because it's interesting or informative.

You wouldn't intentionally run a stop sign, would you? In the same fashion, ignoring warnings may be hazardous to your iPhone and (by extension) your wallet.

Where to Go from Here

Why, straight to Chapter 1, of course (without passing Go).

One final note: At the time we wrote this book, the information it contained was accurate for all iPhone models (including the 3GS, 4/4S, and 5), iOS 6 (the latest version of the iPhone operating system), and the latest version of iTunes (10.7). Apple is likely to introduce a new iPhone model or new versions of the operating system and iTunes between book editions. If you've bought a new iPhone or your version of iTunes looks a little different, be sure to check out what Apple has to say at www.apple.com/iphone.

1

iPhone Basic Training

*I*n addition to being a killer cell phone, the iPhone 5 is a gorgeous widescreen video iPod; a convenient 8-megapixel camera/camcorder; and a small, powerful Internet communications device. With iPhone apps, your iPhone becomes a calendar, an address book, an e-book reader, a handheld gaming device, a memory jogger, an exercise assistant, and ever so much more.

In the following sections, we help you get familiar with this dynamite little device.

Technical Specifications

Before we proceed, here's a list of everything you need before you can actually *use* your iPhone:

- ✔ An iPhone 5

- ✔ In the United States, a wireless contract with AT&T, Sprint or Verizon.

- ✔ An Apple ID (for use with iCloud, the iTunes Store, and the App Store)

- ✔ Internet access (required) — broadband wireless Internet access recommended

To synchronize data with your computer (and download audio and video from your computer's iTunes library), you need the following:

- A Mac with a USB 2.0 or USB 3.0 port; Mac OS X version 10.8 or later; and iTunes 10.7 or later

- A PC with a USB 2.0 port; Windows 7, Windows Vista, or Windows XP Home or Professional with Service Pack 3 or later; and iTunes 10.7 or later

A Quick Tour Outside

The iPhone 5 is a harmonious combination of hardware and software — read on.

On the top and side

On the top of your iPhone 5, you find the sleep/wake button, as shown in Figure 1-1. The SIM card tray is on the top (iPhone 3 and 3GS only) or the side (iPhone 4, 4S, and 5). And the ring/silent switch and the volume buttons are on the side of all versions of the iPhone. We describe these elements more fully in the following list:

- **SIM card tray:** Used to remove or replace the SIM card inside your iPhone.

- **The Sleep/Wake button:** Used to lock or unlock your iPhone and to turn it on or off. When locked, your iPhone can still receive calls and text messages (as well as take pictures with the Camera app), but nothing happens if you touch its screen. When your iPhone is turned off, all incoming calls go directly to voicemail.

- **Ring/Silent switch:** On the left side of the iPhone, this switch enables you to quickly change between ring mode and silent mode. When the switch is set to ring mode — the up position, with no orange strip — your iPhone plays sounds through the speaker on the bottom. When the switch is set to silent mode — the down position, with an orange strip visible on the switch — your iPhone doesn't make a sound when you receive a call or when an alert pops up. You can, however, set your iPhone to vibrate to alert you to an incoming call or notification by going to the Settings app, choosing Sounds, and turning the Vibrate option on.

To silence your phone quickly when in ring mode, press the Sleep/Wake button on the top or one of the Volume buttons.

✔ **Volume buttons:** Found just below the Ring/Silent switch. The upper button increases the volume; the lower one decreases it.

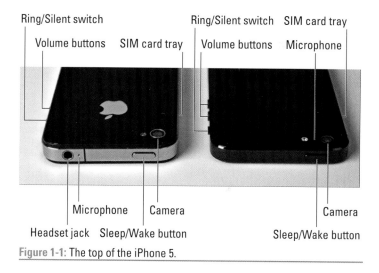

Ring/Silent switch   Ring/Silent switch   SIM card tray

Volume buttons   SIM card tray   Volume buttons   Microphone

Microphone   Camera   Camera

Headset jack   Sleep/Wake button   Sleep/Wake button

Figure 1-1: The top of the iPhone 5.

On the bottom

Here's what you'll find on the bottom of your iPhone (see Figure 1-2):

✔ **Headset jack:** Lets you plug in the included iPhone headset, which has a microphone so that you can talk as well as listen. (The jack is on top of the phone for models that predate the iPhone 5.)

✔ **Microphone:** Lets callers hear your voice when you're not using a headset equipped with a microphone.

✔ **Lightning connector:** Has three purposes. First, use it to recharge your iPhone's battery by connecting one end of the included cable to the Lightning connector and the other end to the USB power adapter. Second, use it to synchronize by connecting one end of the same cable to the Lightning connector and the other end to a USB port on your Mac or PC (this also charges your iPhone, but more slowly than by using the USB power adapter). And third, use the Lightning connector to connect your iPhone to other devices, such as cameras or televisions. (Apple also sells an adapter that converts the Lightning connector to the older 30-pin dock connector used by older iPhone models.)

✔ **Speaker:** Used by the iPhone's built-in speakerphone and plays audio — music or video soundtracks — if no headset is plugged in. It also plays the ringtone you hear when you receive a call.

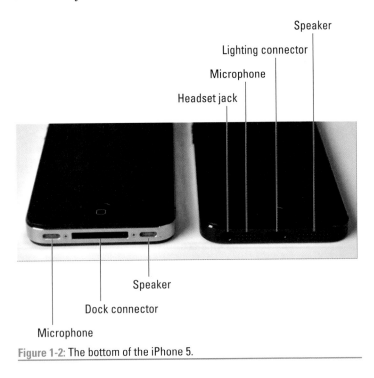

Figure 1-2: The bottom of the iPhone 5.

The iPhone 4 and 4S both have two microphones, whereas the iPhone 5 actually has three. On the iPhone 5, the other microphones are on the back (for use with the Camera app while filming video) and on the front (used for FaceTime calls and to suppress distracting background sounds on calls).

On the front

On the sides and front of your iPhone, you'll find the following (see Figure 1-3):

Figure 1-3: The front of the iPhone is a study in elegant simplicity.

- **Camera (iPhone 4/4S and 5 only):** The camera on the front of the iPhone 4/4S and 5 is tuned for FaceTime, so it has just the right field of view and focal length to focus on your face at arm's length, to present you in the best possible light.

- **Microphone:** The iPhone 5 sports a microphone for use with FaceTime (it also helps suppress ambient noise during calls).

- **Receiver:** The speaker the iPhone uses for telephone calls.

- **Status bar:** At the top of the screen; displays tiny icons that provide a variety of information about the current state of your iPhone.

- **Touchscreen:** See the section "Mastering the Multitouch Interface" later in this chapter for more on using the color touchscreen.

- **Home button:** Press the Home button to display the Home screen.

- **App buttons:** Each button on the Home screen launches an included iPhone app or one you've acquired from the App Store, with one exception. The Utilities button is actually a folder containing four app buttons: Contacts, Calculator, Compass, and Voice Memos. The Utilities button appears only on iPhones that came with iOS 4 (or later) preinstalled. If you upgraded an older iPhone to iOS 4 or 5, or are restoring from a backup, those four apps are still wherever they were before the upgrade.

On the back

On the back of your iPhone is the camera lens. It's the little circle in the top-left corner. The iPhone 4/4S and 5 also have a little LED next to the camera lens that's used as a flash for still photos and as a floodlight for videos, as well as a microphone for recording sound while you're filming video. For more on the camera and shooting video, see Chapters 5 and 6.

Status bar

The status bar is at the top of the screen and displays tiny icons that provide a variety of information about the current state of your iPhone:

Cell signal: Tells you whether you're within range of your wireless telephone carrier's cellular network and therefore can make and receive calls. The more bars the better, of course.

Airplane Mode: You can use your iPod on a plane after the captain gives the word. But you can't use your cell phone except when the plane is in the gate area. Airplane Mode turns off all wireless features of your iPhone so that you can still enjoy music or video during the flight.

3G/4G/LTE: Informs you that the high-speed 3G/4G/LTE data network from your wireless carrier is available; your iPhone can connect to the Internet via any of these data networks.

GPRS: Indicates that your wireless carrier's GPRS data network is available and that your iPhone can use it to connect to the Internet.

EDGE: Indicates that your wireless carrier's EDGE network is available and you can use it to connect to the Internet.

Wi-Fi: Indicates that your iPhone is connected to the Internet over a Wi-Fi network. Again, the more bars that are lit in the familiar Wi-Fi "fan," the better (and likely faster) the connection.

Network activity: Indicates that some network activity is occurring, such as over-the-air synchronization, sending or receiving e-mail, or loading a web page.

Call forwarding: When you see this icon, call forwarding is enabled on your iPhone.

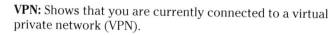

VPN: Shows that you are currently connected to a virtual private network (VPN).

Lock: Shows when your iPhone is locked.

Play: Shows that a song is currently playing.

Portrait orientation: When this icon is displayed, the iPhone is in portrait orientation mode, but not locked in that mode. (See next entry.)

 Portrait orientation lock (iPhone 3GS, 4/4S, and 5 only): This icon means that the iPhone screen is locked in portrait orientation. To lock your screen in portrait orientation, double-press the Home button, flick the dock (at the bottom of the screen) from left to right, and then tap the portrait orientation button.

Alarm: Tells you that you have set one or more alarms in the Clock application.

Location Services: Tells you that some application is using Location Services (see Chapter 8 to learn more).

Bluetooth: Indicates the current state of your iPhone's Bluetooth connection. Blue indicates that Bluetooth is on and a device is connected. Gray indicates that Bluetooth is on but no device is connected.

 Battery: Reflects the level of your battery's charge: completely green when your battery is fully charged and shows a lightning bolt when your iPhone is recharging.

TTY: Informs you that software support for a teletype (TTY) machine for those who are hearing- or speech-impaired is turned on in General Settings; however, TTY requires an external hardware adapter.

Home Sweet Home Screen

Tap the Home button at any time to summon your iPhone's Home screen. The Home screen offers a bevy of icons, each representing a different built-in app or function. This section provides brief descriptions.

 Three steps let you rearrange icons on your iPhone:

1. **Press and hold any icon until all of the icons begin to "wiggle."**

2. **Drag the icons around until you're happy with their positions.**

3. **Press the Home button to save your arrangement and stop the "wiggling."**

If you haven't rearranged your icons, you see the following applications on your Home screen, starting at the top left (iPhones not running iOS 5 or iOS 6 have a different number of icons):

- **Messages:** Lets you exchange text messages with almost any other cell phone via SMS, as well as MMS. You can also take advantage of the iMessage feature in iOS 5 and iOS 6, which enables you to send free text, photo, and video messages to anyone using an Apple device and iOS 5 (or later). This includes other iPhone, iPad, and iPod touch users, as well as anyone with a Mac computer running Mac OS X Lion or Mountain Lion.

- **Calendar:** If you use OS X Calendar; Microsoft Entourage, Outlook, or Exchange; or the online calendars from Google or Yahoo! as your calendar program on your PC or Mac, you can synchronize events and alerts between your computer and your iPhone. Create an event on one and it automatically synchs with the other the next time they're connected (either wirelessly or by cable).

- **Photos:** Indicates the iPhone's terrific photo manager. You can view pictures that you take with the iPhone's built-in cameras or transfer from your computer.

- **Camera:** Lets you shoot a picture with the iPhone's 3-megapixel (iPhone 3GS), 5-megapixel (iPhone 4), or 8-megapixel (iPhone 4S and 5) camera. Ditto if you want to shoot video on the 3GS, 4/4S, or 5 models — the 4S and 5 can even shoot 1080p HD video!

- **Videos:** Speaking of video, tap this icon to watch movies, TV shows, and music videos.

- **Maps:** Lets you view street maps or satellite images of locations around the globe, ask for directions, check traffic conditions, or find a nearby pizza joint.

- **Weather:** Monitors the six-day weather forecast for as many cities as you like.

- **Notes:** Lets you type notes that you can save to your iPhone or e-mail to yourself or anyone else.

- **Reminders:** Saves your to-do list, complete with visual and audio reminders. Find out more in Chapter 7.

✓ **Clock:** Lets you see the current time in as many cities as you like, set one or more alarms, and use your iPhone as a stopwatch or a countdown timer.

✓ **Game Center:** Ready to play a game? The Game Center makes it easy to locate friends for a quick challenge or review your achievements.

✓ **Newsstand:** If you're familiar with iBooks — Apple's e-book reader — you'll feel right at home with this periodical and newspaper reader. (It even updates your subscriptions automatically.)

✓ **iTunes:** Gives you access to the iTunes Store.

✓ **App Store:** Enables you to connect to and search the iTunes App Store for iPhone apps to download.

✓ **Settings:** Lets you adjust your iPhone's settings. Mac users, think System Preferences; Windows users, think Control Panel.

✓ **Passbook:** Stores your airplane boarding passes, event tickets, and store coupons and loyalty cards for easy retrieval. Passbook displays QR and bar codes that can be scanned at event venues and stores.

On the second screen of apps, you now find these two apps that you may be familiar with:

✓ **Stocks:** This app lets you monitor your favorite stocks, which are updated in real time.

✓ **Utilities:** The Utilities icon is actually a folder that contains four utility apps:

  • **Contacts:** Stores information about your contacts.

  • **Calculator:** Lets you perform addition, subtraction, multiplication, and division.

  • **Compass (iPhone 3GS, 4/4S, and 5 only):** Puts a compass inside your iPhone.

  • **Voice Memos:** Turns your iPhone into a convenient handheld recording device.

The Utilities folder appears only on iPhones with iOS 4 (or later) *preinstalled.* iPhones upgraded to iOS 4 won't have this folder.

Finally, the four icons at the bottom of the Home screen are in a special area called the *dock*. When you switch from screen to screen, these icons remain on the screen:

 ✔ **Phone:** Tap this application icon to use the iPhone as a phone!

 ✔ **Mail:** This application lets you send and receive e-mail with most e-mail systems.

 ✔ **Safari:** Lets you surf the web with the Safari web browser.

 ✔ **Music:** Unleashes all the power of a video iPod right on your phone.

Now that you and your iPhone have been properly introduced, it's time to begin using it!

Mastering the Multitouch Interface

The iPhone removes the usual physical buttons in favor of a *multitouch display*. It is the heart of many things you do on the iPhone, and the controls change depending on the task at hand.

The iPhone actually includes six keyboard layouts in English, all variations on the alphabetical keyboard, the numeric and punctuation keyboard, and the more punctuation and symbols keyboard. The layout you see on your iPhone depends on the application you are working in. The keyboards in Safari, for example, differ from those in Notes.

The iPhone keyboard contains five keys that don't actually type a character: Shift, Toggle, International keyboard, Delete, and Return:

 ✔ **Shift key:** If you're using the alphabetical keyboard, the Shift key switches between uppercase and lowercase letters. If you're using either of the other two keyboards, pressing Shift switches to the one you're not currently using.

To turn on Caps Lock and type in all caps, you first need to enable Caps Lock. Tap the Settings icon, tap General, and then tap Keyboard. Tap the Enable Caps Lock item to turn it on. After the Caps Lock setting is enabled (it's disabled by default), you double-tap the Shift key to turn on Caps Lock. (The Shift key turns blue when Caps Lock is on.) Tap the Shift key again to turn off Caps Lock. To disable Caps Lock completely, just reverse the process by turning off the Enable Caps Lock setting (tap Settings, General, Keyboard).

- **Toggle key:** Switches between the different keyboard layouts.

- **International keyboard key:** Shows up only if you've turned on an international keyboard.

- **Delete key:** Erases the character immediately to the left of the cursor.

- **Return key:** Moves the cursor to the beginning of the next line.

The virtual iPhone keyboard

Here's why this keyboard is so smart:

- Includes a built-in English dictionary with words from today's popular culture.

- Adds your contacts to its dictionary automatically.

- Uses complex analysis algorithms to predict the word you're trying to type.

- Suggests corrections as you type. It then offers you the suggested word just below the misspelled word. When you decline a suggestion and the word you typed is *not* in the iPhone dictionary, the iPhone adds that word to its dictionary and offers it as a suggestion in the future.

Remember to decline suggestions (by tapping the characters you typed as opposed to the suggested words that appear beneath what you've typed), as doing so helps your intelligent keyboard become even smarter.

- Reduces the number of mistakes you make as you type by intelligently and dynamically resizing the touch zones for certain keys.

Training your digits

Using the iPhone efficiently means that you need to master a few tricks: Tap, flick, swipe, and pinch:

- **Tap:** Tapping serves multiple purposes. Tap an icon to open an application from the Home screen, to start playing a song or to choose the photo album you want to look through. Sometimes you double-tap (twice in rapid succession) to zoom in (or out of) web pages, maps, and e-mails.

- **Flick:** A flick of the finger on the screen lets you quickly scroll through lists of songs, e-mails, and picture thumbnails. Tap on the screen to stop scrolling, or merely wait for the scrolling list to stop.

- **Swipe:** Swipe downward from the top of the screen — all it takes is one finger — and your iPhone displays the Notification Center, where you can track all notifications you've received (including calls and voicemails, messages displayed by apps, and even weather and stock figures). Many apps also allow you to browse photos and screens by swiping left and right across your screen.

- **Pinch/spread:** Place two fingers on the edges of a web page or picture to enlarge the images or make them smaller. Pinching and spreading are easy to master.

The Home screen discussed earlier in this chapter may not be the only screen of icons on your phone. When you start adding apps from the App Store, you may see two or more tiny dots between the Phone, Mail, Safari, and Music icons and the row of icons directly above them. These dots denote additional screens.

The white dot indicates the screen you're currently viewing. To navigate between screens, either flick from right to left or left to right across the middle of the screen or tap directly on the dots. At the far end of this row of dots you can see a small magnifying glass. Tapping this icon triggers the Spotlight search feature (discussed in more detail at the end of this chapter).

Press the Home button to jump back to the first screen of icons or the Home screen. Pressing Home a second time brings you to the handy Spotlight search feature.

If you press the Home button twice in rapid succession, your iPhone displays the multitasking bar, where the apps that you've used recently (and those that are still running in the background) are conveniently displayed. To close the bar, either tap one of the app icons or press the Home button again.

Finger-typing

If you're patient and trusting, you'll get the hang of finger-typing in a week or so. You have to rely on the virtual keyboard that appears when you tap a text field to enter notes, compose text messages, type the names of new contacts, and so forth.

The keyboard does a pretty good job of coming up with the words you have in mind. As you press your finger against a letter or number on the screen, the individual key you press gets bigger and practically jumps off the screen, as shown in Figure 1-4. That way, you know that you struck the correct letter or number.

Figure 1-4: The ABCs of virtual typing.

Mistakes are common at first. Say that you meant to type a sentence in the Notes application that reads, "I am typing a bunch of notes." But because of the way your fingers struck the virtual keys, you actually entered "I am typing a bunch of *niyrs.*" Fortunately, Apple knows that the *o* you meant to press is next to the *i* that showed up on the keyboard, just as *t* and *y* and the *e* and the *r* are side by side. So the software determines that *notes* was indeed the word you had in mind and places it in red under the suspect word, as shown in Figure 1-5. To accept the suggested word, merely tap the Space key. And if for some reason you actually did mean to type *npyrs* instead, tap on the suggested word (*notes* in this example) to decline it.

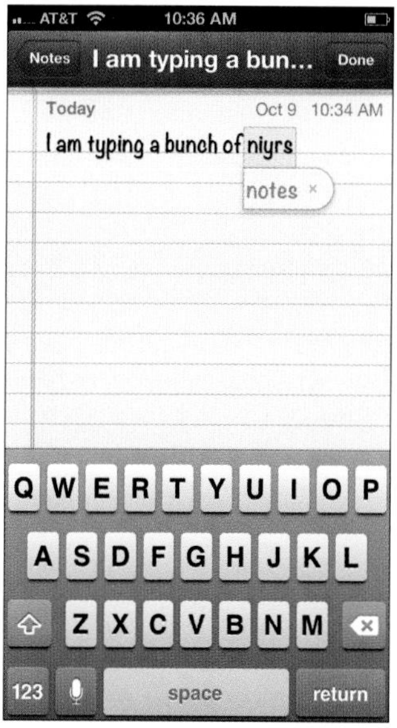

Figure 1-5: When the keyboard bails you out.

When you're typing notes or sending e-mail and want to type a number, symbol, or punctuation mark, tap the *123* key to bring up an alternative virtual keyboard. Tap the *ABC* key to return to the first keyboard. And when you're in Safari, if you press and hold the .com key, you are offered the choice of .com, .net, .edu, or .org.

You can rotate the iPhone so that its keyboard changes to a wider landscape mode, with slightly larger keys, in most iPhone apps (including Mail, Messages, Notes, Reminders, and Safari).

Don't forget: if you're using an iPhone 4S or 5, you can eschew the keyboard completely and use your voice to dictate messages, notes, and reminders to *Siri* (the iPhone voice assistant). See Chapter 4 to learn about Siri. (You can also use the Dictation feature without invoking Siri. The Dictation key is to the left of the Space key — you can tap it any time you'd normally be typing (like within the body of an e-mail message or a text message) and then begin speaking. Tap the Done button to exit Dictation mode.)

Editing mistakes

It's a good idea to type with reckless abandon and not get hung up over the characters you mistype. Again, the self-correcting keyboard will fix many errors. That said, plenty of typos will likely turn up, especially in the beginning, and you'll have to make corrections manually.

A neat trick for doing so is to hold your finger against the screen to bring up the magnifying glass shown in Figure 1-6. Use it to position the pointer to the spot where you need to make the correction.

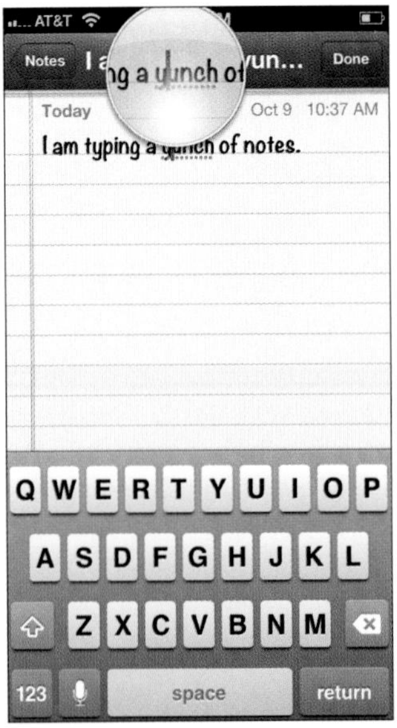

![Screenshot of iPhone Notes app with magnifying glass over the text "I am typing a bunch of notes." and an on-screen keyboard below]

Figure 1-6: Magnifying errors.

Using Cut, Copy, Paste, and Replace

Being able to copy and paste text (or images) from one place on a computer to another has seemingly been a divine right since Moses. Of course, Apple provides Copy and Paste (and Cut) on the iPhone, as well as another remedy for correcting errors: the Replace pop-up option.

On the iPhone, you might copy text or images from the web and paste them into text, an e-mail, a message, or a note. Or you might copy a bunch of pictures or video into an e-mail.

Here's how to exploit the feature. Let's assume you're jotting down ideas in Notes that you want to copy into an e-mail:

1. **Double-tap a word to select it.**

2. **Drag the blue grab points to expand the highlighted text block (see Figure 1-7). After you select the text, tap Copy. (If you want to delete the text block, tap Cut instead.)**

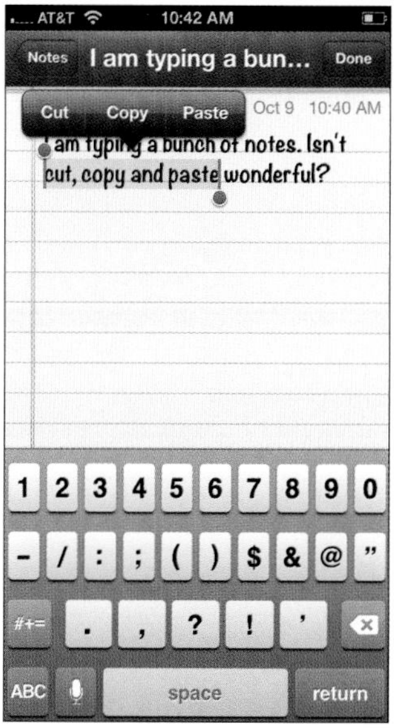

Figure 1-7: Drag the grab points to select text.

3. **Open the Mail program and start composing a message.**

4. **Insert the text you just copied into your e-mail message by tapping the cursor. Commands to Select, Select All, and Paste pop up, as shown in Figure 1-8.**

5. **Tap Paste to paste the text into the message.**

Figure 1-8: Tap Paste to insert the text you copied.

Any time you notice an error in text you've typed or pasted, you can double-tap the word and the options change to Cut, Copy, Paste, and Replace. Tap Replace, and the iPhone serves up a few suggested replacement words. If the word you want to substitute is listed, tap it, and the iPhone automatically makes the switch. If you make a mistake while typing or editing, simply shake the iPhone to undo the last edit.

Organizing with Folders

Finding the single app you want to use among apps spread out across 11 screens is a daunting task. Never fear, Apple includes a handy organization tool called Folders. This feature enables you to create folder icons, each holding up to a dozen apps.

To create a folder, press your finger against an icon until all the icons on the screen jiggle. Decide which apps you want to move to a folder, and drag the icon for the first app on top of the second app. The two apps now share living quarters inside a newly created folder. Apple names the folder according to the category of apps inside the folder, but you can easily change the folder name by tapping the X in the bar where the folder name appears and substituting a new name.

To launch an app that's inside a folder, tap that folder's icon and then tap the icon for the app that you want to open.

You can drag apps into and out of any folder as long as there's room for them — remember that you can have no more than 12 apps in a folder. But your iPhone can have as many as 180 folders, with a total of 2,160 apps.

If you drag all the apps outside the folder, the folder automatically disappears.

Searching with Spotlight

Using the Safari browser, you can search the web via Google, Yahoo!, or Microsoft Bing. But what if you need to search for people and programs across your iPhone?

Searching across the iPhone is based on the Spotlight feature familiar to Mac owners. To access Spotlight, flick to the left of the main Home screen (or as mentioned earlier in this chapter, press the Home button from the Home screen).

In the bar at the top of the screen that slides into view, enter your search query using the virtual keyboard. The iPhone starts spitting out results the moment you type a single character, and the list gets narrowed each time you type an additional character. The results are pretty darn thorough.

2

Getting Stuff to and from Your iPhone

*A*fter you understand the basics (see Chapter 1), you probably want to get some or all of the following into your iPhone: contacts, appointments, events, mail settings, bookmarks, ringtones, music, movies, TV shows, podcasts, audio and e-books, courseware, photos, documents, and applications.

The good news is that you can easily copy any or all of those items from your computer to your iPhone. After you do that, you can synchronize your contacts, appointments, and events so they're kept up-to-date automatically everywhere you might need them — on your computer, iPhone, iPad, and iPod touch. So when you add or change an appointment, an event, or a contact on your iPhone, that information automatically appears on your computer and other devices.

This communication between your iPhone and computer is called *syncing* (short for synchronizing). Don't worry; syncing is easy, and we walk you through the entire process in this chapter.

Here's even more good news: iOS 5 and iOS 6 are PC-free, which means you don't *have* to connect your iPhone to a computer running iTunes. In this chapter, you discover how to sync both with and without connecting your iPhone to a computer. But bear in mind that certain tasks — such as rearranging icons on your Home screens and managing media — are easier on a computer than on the iPhone's smaller screen.

This chapter also introduces iCloud, which can automatically transfer data from your iPhone to other iOS 5 (or later) devices and your Mac and back again. (It even works with PCs.) Apple calls this exchange *pushing.* Whenever you buy a new song or book on your iPhone, for example, it is pushed wirelessly to your computer and your iPad through iCloud.

The information in this chapter is based on iTunes version 10.7 and iOS version 6, which were the latest and greatest when these words were written. If your screens don't look like ours, upgrade to iTunes 10.7 or higher (choose iTunes⇨Check for Updates), to iOS 6 or higher (click the Check for Update button on the Summary tab shown in the upcoming Figure 2-2 and follow the instructions for updating your iPhone), or both. Both upgrades are free and offer useful new features that have significant advantages over their predecessors.

Setting Up a New iPhone

Here are the steps for setting up a brand-new iPhone:

1. **Turn on the iPhone or wake it if it's sleeping.**

   The first thing you see on a new iPhone is the Language Selection screen.

2. **Tap the language you want this iPhone to use and move to the next screen.**

   Tap the blue arrow button in the upper-right corner to advance to the next screen.

3. **Tap your country or region and then tap the blue Next button.**

4. **Tap to enable or disable Location Services and then tap the blue Next button.**

   Location Services is your iPhone's way of knowing your precise geographical location. The Maps app, for example, which is covered in Chapter 8, relies on Location Services to determine where in the world you are.

5. **Tap to choose a Wi-Fi network, type a password if necessary, tap the blue Join button, and then tap the blue Next button.**

   Tapping Next initiates the activation process, which requires either a Wi-Fi network or your wireless carrier's cellular network and may take up to five minutes.

   If neither network is available, you see an alert that says you need to connect your iPhone to your computer and use iTunes to complete the activation and setup process, as described in the first four steps in "The Kitchen Sync" section, later in this chapter.

   After your iPhone has been activated, the Set Up iPhone screen appears.

6. **Do one of the following:**

   • **If this is your first iPhone:** You won't have any backups yet, so choose Set Up as New iPhone and tap the blue Next button. The Apple ID screen appears.

   • **If you're replacing an old iPhone with this one:** Choose either Restore from iCloud Backup or Restore from iTunes Backup to have the new iPhone restored with the settings and data from your previous one. You see either the iCloud Sign In screen or the Connect to iTunes screen. Follow the on-screen instructions and choose the backup you want to restore from. In a few minutes (or more if your old iPhone contained a lot of data), your new iPhone will contain all the apps, media files, and settings from your old iPhone. You're finished and can skip ahead to the next section, "A Brief iCloud Primer."

7. **Tap Sign In with Your Apple ID or tap Create a Free Apple ID. Then (you know) tap the blue Next button.**

   You can tap Skip This Step and proceed without supplying an Apple ID, but we strongly advise against that choice. You need a free Apple ID to take advantage of myriad excellent and free features — including iCloud — described in this and other chapters

   The Terms and Conditions screen appears.

8. **To agree to the terms and conditions, tap the blue Agree button in the lower-right corner.**

   A Terms and Conditions alert appears.

9. **Tap the Agree button and then tap the blue Next button.**

   What happens if you disagree? You don't want to know. And, of course, you won't be able to use your iPhone.

   The Set Up iCloud screen appears.

10. **Do one of the following:**

    • **If you want to use iCloud:** Good choice! Tap Use iCloud and then tap the blue Next button. Follow the instructions on the Back Up to iCloud screen and tap the blue Next button again.

    If you're committed to using your iPhone PC-free, we urge you to use iCloud to back up your iPhone.

    • **If you don't want to use iCloud:** Tap Don't Use iCloud and then tap the blue arrow button.

    The Find My iPhone screen appears next.

11. **Tap Use Find My iPhone or Don't Use Find My iPhone, and then tap the blue Next button.**

    Find My iPhone is a seriously cool feature that lets you locate and secure (even remotely wipe) your iPhone if it ever gets lost or stolen.

    If you don't have an iPhone 4S or 5, skip the next step.

12. **If you have an iPhone 4S or 5, tap Use Siri or Don't Use Siri and then tap the blue Next button.**

Siri is an intelligent, voice-controlled assistant available only on the iPhone 4S and 5.

We can't think of a good reason not to enable Siri, but if that's your choice, you can still use voice commands for dialing the phone and controlling the Music app.

The Diagnostics screen appears.

13. **Tap either Automatically Send or Don't Send, and then tap the blue Next button.**

    If you tap Automatically Send, anonymous diagnostic and usage data will be sent to Apple.

    The Thank You screen appears.

14. **Tap Start Using iPhone to, well, start using your iPhone.**

    Your iPhone's Home screen appears in all its glory.

Finally, although Apple's free iCloud wireless storage and synchronization service (described in the following section) is strictly optional, it's especially useful if you're planning to use your iPhone PC-free.

A Brief iCloud Primer

Apple's iCloud service is more than just a wireless hard drive in the sky. Rather, iCloud is a complete wireless storage and data synchronization solution. In a nutshell, iCloud is designed to store and manage your digital stuff — your music, photos, contacts, bookmarks, events, and more — keeping everything updated on all your computers and i-devices automatically with no physical (wired) connection or action on your part. Like so many things Apple makes, iCloud just works.

iCloud pushes information such as e-mail, calendars, contacts, and bookmarks to and from your computer and to and from your iPhone and other i-devices and then keeps those items updated on all devices, wirelessly and without human intervention. iCloud also includes nonsynchronizing options, such as Photo Stream (see Chapter 6) and e-mail (see Chapter 7).

Your free iCloud account includes 5GB of free storage, which is all many (if not most) users need. If you find yourself needing more storage, 15-, 25-, and 55GB upgrades are available for $20, $40, and $100 a year, respectively.

A nice touch is that music, apps, books, periodicals, movies, and TV shows you purchase from the iTunes Store, as well as your Photo Stream, don't count against your 5GB of free storage. You'll find that the things that do count — such as mail, documents, photos taken with your iPhone camera, account information, settings, and other app data — don't use much space, so that 5GB should last you a long time.

If you plan to go PC-free but want to have your e-mail, calendars, contacts, and bookmarks synchronized automatically and wirelessly (and believe us, you do), here's how to enable iCloud syncing on your iPhone:

1. **Tap Settings on your Home screen.**

2. **Tap iCloud in the list of settings.**

3. **Tap Account and provide your Apple ID and password.**

4. **Tap Done.**

Now tap any of the individual On/Off switches to enable or disable iCloud sync for any of the following options:

- Mail
- Contacts
- Calendars
- Reminders
- Safari Bookmarks
- Notes
- Passbook
- Photo Stream
- Documents & Data
- Find My iPhone

You find out much more about iCloud in the rest of this chapter, so let's move on to syncing your iPhone.

The Kitchen Sync

If you're using your iPhone PC-free because you don't own or have access to a computer, you can skip the rest of the chapter. Why? If you don't have a computer, you don't have any data or media to sync with your iPhone, so you can skip ahead to Chapter 3 now.

Sync prep 101

For those who want to sync, either with the included Lightning connector–to–USB cable or wirelessly over Wi-Fi, follow the instructions in the rest of this chapter. Even if you want to sync wirelessly, you have to connect your iPhone to your computer with a cable just this once; when you've completed the syncing setup, you won't need to use the cable again.

So, unless you don't have a computer at all, just follow these steps and you'll be ready to sync via cable or wirelessly in just a few minutes:

1. **Start by connecting your iPhone to your computer with the Lightning connector–to–USB cable included with your iPhone.**

   When you connect your iPhone to your computer, iTunes should launch automatically. If it doesn't, chances are you plugged the cable into a USB port on your keyboard, monitor, or hub. Try plugging it into one of the USB ports on your computer instead. Why? Because USB ports on your computer supply more power to a connected device than other USB ports or most hubs.

   If iTunes still doesn't launch automatically, try launching it manually.

   One last thing: If you've taken any photos with your iPhone since the last time you synced it, your photo management software (iPhoto, Dropbox, Image Capture, or Aperture on the Mac; Adobe Photoshop Elements or Dropbox on the PC) launches and asks whether you want to import the photos from your phone. (You find out all about this in the "Photos" section, later in the chapter.)

If you don't see an iPhone in the source list, and you're sure your iPhone is connected to a USB port on your computer (not on the keyboard, monitor, or hub), try restarting your computer.

2. **Select your iPhone in the iTunes source list.**

   If you're setting up this iPhone for the first time, you see the Set Up Your iPhone pane shown in Figure 2-1. If you've already named your iPhone, skip to Step 5.

Figure 2-1: This is the first thing you see in iTunes.

3. **Name your iPhone.**

   We've named this one *BobLiPhone.*

4. **Choose what, if anything, you want iTunes to automatically synchronize and then click Done.**

   You can sync only your iPhone, or you can sync only your contacts, calendars, bookmarks, notes, e-mail accounts, and apps, or you can sync everything.

   However, we suggest that you leave both boxes unchecked and set everything up manually, as described in the remainder of this section. That way, you'll see additional options for syncing contacts, calendars, bookmarks, notes, e-mail accounts, and apps, as well as how to sync media including movies, TV shows, and podcasts.

5. **Click the Summary tab near the top of the window, as shown in Figure 2-2.**

   If you don't see a Summary tab, make sure your iPhone is still selected in the source list.

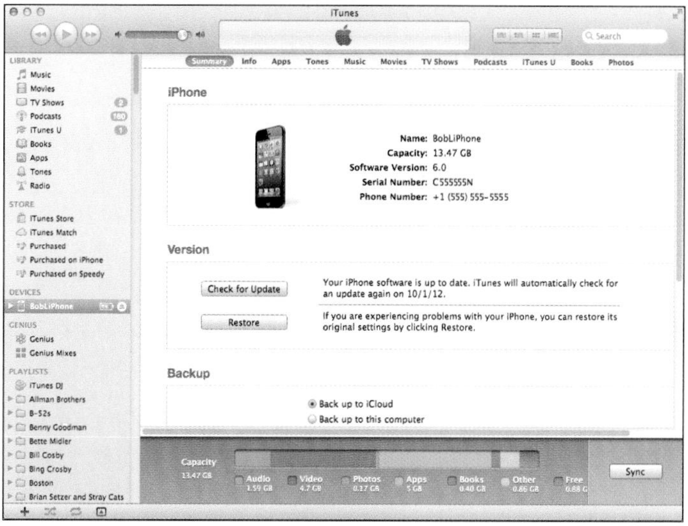

Figure 2-2: The Summary pane is pretty painless.

6. **Click Back Up to iCloud or Back Up to This Computer in the Backup section of the Summary pane.**

   Your iPhone creates a backup of its contents automatically every time you sync, regardless of whether you sync using a USB cable or wirelessly.

   If you choose to store your backups locally, on your computer, you can encrypt and password-protect them by selecting the Encrypt iPhone Backup check box section.

   You can always start an iCloud Backup manually by tapping Settings⟹iCloud⟹ Storage & Backup ⟹ Back Up Now.

   That's all there is to the Backup section. The remaining steps deals with the check boxes in the Options section (refer to Figure 2-2).

7. **If you want iTunes to launch automatically and sync your iPhone whenever you connect it to your computer, click to put a check mark in the Open iTunes When This iPhone Is Connected check box (in the Options section).**

If the Prevent iPods, iPhones, and iPads from Syncing Automatically option in the Devices pane of iTunes Preferences (iTunes➪Preferences on a Mac; Edit➪Preferences on a PC) is enabled (checked), the Open iTunes When This iPhone Is Connected option in the Summary tab is disabled.

Your choice in this step is not set in stone. If you select the Open iTunes When This iPhone Is Connected check box, you can still prevent your iPhone from syncing automatically in two ways:

- **Way #1:** After you connect the iPhone to your computer, click the Summary tab in iTunes and deselect the Open iTunes When This iPhone Is Connected check box. Removing the check mark prevents iTunes from opening automatically when you connect the iPhone. If you use this method, you can still sync manually by clicking the Sync button.

- **Way #2:** Launch iTunes *before* you connect your iPhone to your computer. Then press and hold Command+Option (Mac) or Shift+Ctrl (PC) and connect your iPhone. Keep pressing the keys until you see your iPhone appear in the iTunes source list. This method prevents your iPhone from syncing automatically without changing any settings.

8. **If you want to sync automatically over your Wi-Fi connection, select the Sync with This iPhone over Wi-Fi check box.**

You can also configure your iPhone to allow automatic downloads of music, apps, and books that you install on other iOS 5 and iOS 6 devices. Tap the Settings icon on the Home screen and then tap the iTunes & App Stores item. Enable each of the media types that you want to automatically receive on your iPhone.

9. **If you want to sync only items that have check marks to the left of their names in your iTunes library, select the Sync Only Checked Songs and Videos check box.**

10. **If you want high-definition videos you import to be automatically converted into smaller standard-definition video files when you transfer them to your iPhone, select the Prefer Standard Definition Videos check box.**

    Standard-definition video files are significantly smaller than high-definition video files. You'll hardly notice the difference when you watch the video on your iPhone, but you can have more video files on your iPhone because they take up less space.

    That said, if you choose to watch video from your iPhone on an HDTV either with one of the A/V adapters mentioned next or wirelessly via AirPlay, you'll definitely notice a big difference.

    If you plan to use Apple's Digital A/V Adapter, Component A/V Cable ($39 each — at press time tune this option also required purchasing the $29 Lightning-to-30-pin adapter — it's expected that Apple will release an updated cable in the near future), or Apple TV ($99) to display movies on an HDTV, consider going with high definition. Although the files will be bigger and your iPhone will hold fewer videos, the HD versions look spectacular on a big-screen TV.

    Finally, if you have a wireless network at home, you don't need to sync video you intend to watch at home with your iPhone. Instead, you can stream it to your iPhone or HDTV with an Apple TV.

    The conversion from HD to standard definition takes a *long* time, so be prepared for very long sync times when you sync new HD video and have this option enabled.

11. **If you want iTunes to automatically create smaller-size audio files (so you can fit more music on your iPhone), select the Convert Higher Bit Rate Songs to AAC check box.**

    By default, the bit rate is 128 kbps. Click the pop-up list to specify the bit rate for the target songs.

12. **If you want to turn off automatic syncing in just the Music and Video panes, select the Manually Manage Music and Videos check box.**

And, of course, if you decide not to select the Open iTunes When This iPhone Is Connected check box, you can synchronize manually by clicking the Sync button in the bottom-right corner of the window. Note, however, that if you've changed any sync settings since the last time you synchronized, the Sync button will say Apply instead of Sync.

Syncing Your Data

Did you choose to set up data synchronization manually (by not selecting the Automatically Sync Contacts, Calendars, Bookmarks, Notes, and Email Accounts check box or the Automatically Sync Applications check box in the Set Up Your iPhone pane shown in Figure 2-1)? If you did, your next order of business is to tell iTunes what data you want to synchronize between your iPhone and your computer. You do this by clicking the Info tab, which is to the right of the Summary tab.

The Info pane has five sections: Sync Contacts, Sync Calendars, Sync Mail Accounts, Other, and Advanced. The following sections look at them one by one.

If you are using iCloud to sync contacts, calendars, bookmarks, or notes, DO NOT enable those items in iTunes, as we're about to describe. There's a warning in fine print at the bottom of each section that says so, but some folks don't read the fine print, so here's our warning in bold type: **If you enable syncing with iCloud and also enable it in iTunes, you may end up with duplicated data on your iPhone.** We guarantee you won't like that, so enable syncing one way or the other — via iCloud *or* in the iTunes Info pane.

Syncing contacts

The Sync Contacts section of the Info pane determines how synchronization is handled for your contacts. One method is to synchronize all your contacts, as shown in Figure 2-3. Or you can synchronize any or all groups of contacts you've created in your computer's address book program; just select the appropriate check boxes in the Selected Groups list, and only those groups will be synchronized.

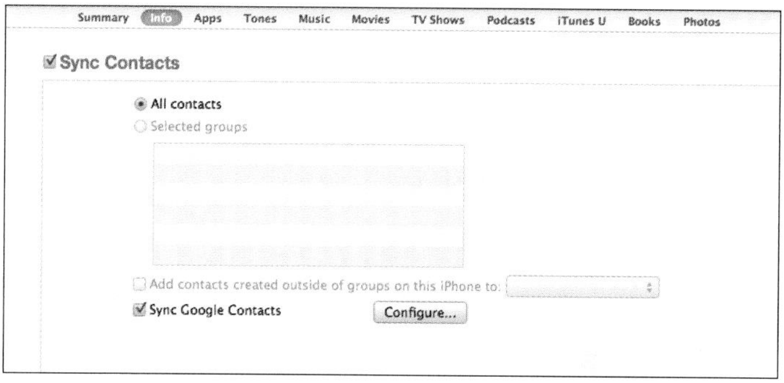

Figure 2-3: Want to synchronize your contacts? This is where you set things up.

The iPhone syncs with the following address book programs:

- **Mac:** Contacts and other address books that sync with the Contacts app, such as Microsoft Outlook 2011 or the now discontinued Microsoft Entourage

- **PC:** Windows Contacts (Vista and Windows 7), Windows Addressbook (XP), Microsoft Outlook, and Microsoft Outlook Express

- **Mac and PC:** Yahoo! Address Book and Google Contacts

Now, here's what each option in the Sync Contacts section does:

- **All Contacts:** One method is to synchronize all your contacts, as shown in Figure 2-3. This synchronizes every contact in your Mac Contacts application or PC address book with your iPhone's Contacts app.

- **Selected Groups:** You can synchronize any or all groups of contacts you've created in your computer's address book program. Just select the appropriate check boxes in the Selected Groups list, and only those groups are synchronized.

✔ **Yahoo! or Google Contacts:** If you use Yahoo! Address Book, select the Sync Yahoo! Address Book Contacts check box and then click the Configure button to enter your Yahoo! ID and password. If you use Google Contacts, select the Sync Google Contacts check box and then click the Configure button to enter your Google ID and password.

If you use Yahoo!, note that syncing doesn't delete a contact from your Yahoo! Address Book if the contact has a Yahoo! Messenger ID, even if you delete that contact on the iPhone or on your computer. To delete a contact that has a Yahoo! Messenger ID, log on to your Yahoo! account with a web browser and delete the contact in your Yahoo! Address Book.

If you sync with your employer's Microsoft Exchange calendar and contacts, any personal contacts or calendars already on your iPhone will be wiped out.

Syncing calendars

The Calendars section of the Info pane determines how synchronization is handled for your appointments and events. You can synchronize all your calendars, as shown in Figure 2-4. Or you can synchronize any or all individual calendars you've created in your computer's calendar program. Just select the appropriate check boxes.

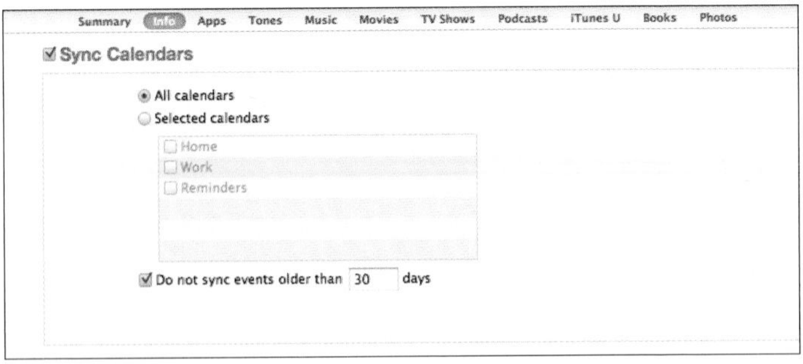

Summary	Info	Apps	Tones	Music	Movies	TV Shows	Podcasts	iTunes U	Books	Photos

☑ Sync Calendars

⦿ All calendars
◯ Selected calendars

☐ Home
☐ Work
☐ Reminders

☑ Do not sync events older than 30   days

Figure 2-4: Set up sync for your calendar events here.

The Calendars section is named Sync Calendars because Figure 2-4 was captured in iTunes for the Mac. If you use a PC, this section is named Sync Calendars with Outlook. As before, don't worry — regardless of its name, it works the same on either platform.

The iPhone syncs with the following calendar programs:

- **Mac:** OS X Calendar, plus any tasks or events that currently sync with Calendar on your Mac

- **PC:** Microsoft Outlook 2003, 2007, and 2010

- **Mac and PC:** Google and Yahoo! Calendars

Syncing e-mail accounts

You can sync account settings for your e-mail accounts in the Sync Mail Accounts section of the Info pane. You can synchronize all your e-mail accounts (if you have more than one) or individual accounts, as shown in Figure 2-5. Just select the appropriate check boxes.

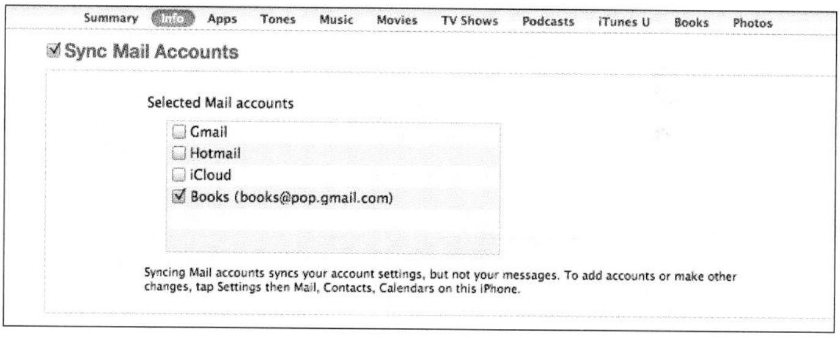

| Summary | **Info** | Apps | Tones | Music | Movies | TV Shows | Podcasts | iTunes U | Books | Photos |

☑ **Sync Mail Accounts**

Selected Mail accounts

☐ Gmail
☐ Hotmail
☐ iCloud
☑ Books (books@pop.gmail.com)

Syncing Mail accounts syncs your account settings, but not your messages. To add accounts or make other changes, tap Settings then Mail, Contacts, Calendars on this iPhone.

Figure 2-5: Transfer e-mail account settings to your iPhone here.

The iPhone syncs with the following mail programs:

- **Mac:** Mail

- **PC:** Microsoft Outlook 2003, 2007, 2010 and Microsoft Outlook Express

- **Mac and PC:** Gmail and Yahoo! Mail

E-mail account settings are synchronized only one way: from your computer to your iPhone. If you make changes to any e-mail account settings on your iPhone, the changes are *not* synchronized back to the e-mail account on your computer. Trust us, this is a very good feature, and we're glad Apple did it this way.

By the way, the password for your e-mail account may or may not be saved on your computer. If you sync an e-mail account and the iPhone asks for a password when you send or receive mail, do this: On the Home screen, tap Settings, and then tap Mail, Contacts, Calendars. Tap your e-mail account's name, tap it again on the following screen, and then type your password in the appropriate field.

Syncing bookmarks and notes

The settings available in the Other section of the Info pane vary depending on whether you're syncing using iCloud or syncing over a cable/Wi-Fi connection. If you're syncing using iCloud, there are actually no settings to make in this section. If you're syncing over cable, however, you can select the Sync Safari Bookmarks check box if you want to sync the bookmarks on your computer with bookmarks on your iPhone. The iPhone can sync bookmarks with the following web browsers:

- **Mac:** Safari
- **PC:** Microsoft Internet Explorer and Safari

Advanced syncing

Every so often, the contacts, calendars, or mail accounts on your iPhone get so screwed up that the easiest way to fix things is to erase that information on your iPhone and replace it with information from your computer.

If that's the case, just click to select the appropriate check boxes in the Advanced section of the Info pane, as shown in Figure 2-6. Then the next time you sync, that information on your iPhone will be replaced with information from your computer.

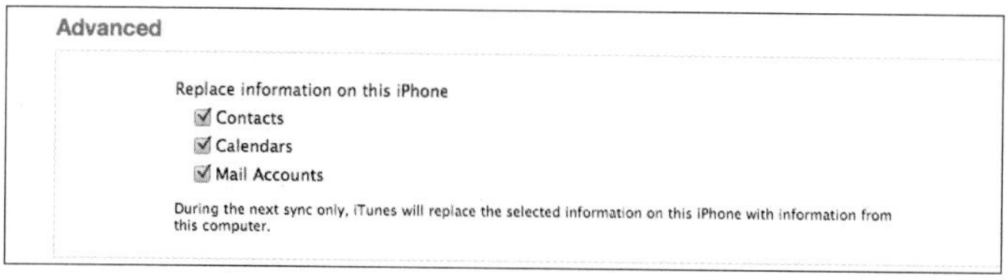

Advanced

Replace information on this iPhone
☑ Contacts
☑ Calendars
☑ Mail Accounts

During the next sync only, iTunes will replace the selected information on this iPhone with information from this computer.

Figure 2-6: Replace the information on your iPhone with the information on your computer.

Because the Advanced section is at the bottom of the Info pane and you have to scroll down to see it, it's easy to forget that it's there. Although you probably won't need to use this feature very often (if ever), you'll be happy you remembered that it's there if you do need it.

One last thing: Check boxes in the Advanced section are disabled for items not selected, as described in the previous sections (Contacts, Calendars, and Mail Accounts in Figure 2-6). If you're using iCloud and you want to replace any of these items on your iPhone, you must first enable that item as discussed in the previous sections of this chapter. In other words, if you want to replace Contacts, Calendars, or Mail Accounts in Figure 2-6, you first have to select Sync Contacts, Sync Calendars, and Sync Mail Accounts, as just described.

Synchronizing Your Media

If you chose to let iTunes manage synchronizing your data automatically, welcome back. This section looks at how you get your media — your ringtones, music, movies, TV shows, podcasts, video, iTunes U courses, books, and photos — from your computer to your iPhone.

Sharp-eyed readers may notice that we aren't covering syncing iPhone apps in this chapter. Apps are so darn cool that we've given them an entire chapter, namely Chapter 9. In that chapter, you discover how to find and sync apps, and much, much more.

Ringtones, music, podcasts, iTunes U courses, books, and video (but not photos) are synced in only one direction: from your computer to your iPhone. If you delete any of these items on your iPhone, they are not deleted from your computer when you sync. If you purchase or download items directly to your iPhone using the iTunes app or App Store app, those items (that is, songs, ringtones, podcasts, video, iTunes U courses, and books) are synced back to your computer when your iPhone syncs. And if you delete anything you've purchased — movies, songs, TV shows, or whatever — you can download them to your iPhone at no charge with the iTunes or App Store app's Purchased section.

Ringtones, music, movies, and TV shows

You use the Tones, Music, Movies, TV Shows, Podcasts, and iTunes U panes to specify the media that you want to copy from your computer to your iPhone. To view any of these panes, make sure that your iPhone is still selected in the source list, and then click the appropriate tab near the top of the window.

Ringtones

If you have custom ringtones in your iTunes library, select the Sync Tones check box in the Tones pane. Then you can choose either all ringtones or individual ringtones by selecting their check boxes.

Ringtones can also be used as text tones.

Music, music videos, and voice memos

To transfer music to your iPhone, select the Sync Music check box in the Music pane. You can then select the option for Entire Music Library or Selected Playlists, Artists, and Genres. If you choose the latter, click the check boxes next to particular playlists, artists, and genres you want to transfer. You also can choose to include music videos or voice memos or both by selecting the appropriate check boxes at the top of the pane (see Figure 2-7).

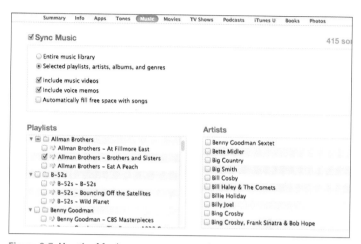

Figure 2-7: Use the Music pane to copy music, music videos, and voice memos from your computer to your iPhone.

If none of the options just mentioned sounds just right (pun intended), you can drag individual songs onto the Manually Added Songs section near the bottom of the Music pane.

If you choose Entire Music Library and have more songs in your iTunes library than storage space on your iPhone, you see one or both of the error messages shown in Figure 2-8 when you try to sync. You also see a yellow alert on the right side of the Capacity chart at the bottom of the screen, along with how much over your iPhone's capacity adding the entire music library would make you. To avoid such errors, select playlists, artists, and genres that total less than the free space on your iPhone, which is also displayed in the Capacity chart at the bottom of the iTunes screen.

Music, podcasts, and video are notorious for using massive amounts of storage space on your iPhone. If you try to sync too much media, you'll see lots of error messages like the ones in Figure 2-8. Forewarned is forearmed.

Finally, if you select the Automatically Fill Free Space with Songs check box, iTunes fills any free space on your iPhone with music.

Figure 2-8: If you have more music than your iPhone has room for, this is what you'll see when you sync.

Movies

To transfer movies to your iPhone, select the Sync Movies check box and then choose an option for movies you want to include automatically from the pop-up menu, as shown in Figure 2-9. If you choose an option other than All, you can optionally select individual movies and playlists by checking the boxes in appropriate sections.

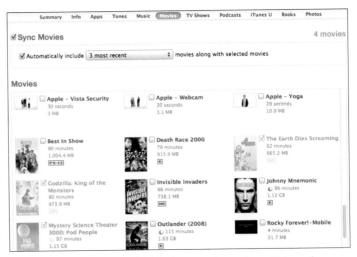

Figure 2-9: Your choices in the Movies pane determine which movies are copied to your iPhone.

TV shows

The procedure for syncing TV shows is slightly different from the procedure for syncing movies. First, select the Sync TV Shows check box to enable TV show syncing. Then choose how many episodes to include and whether you want all shows or only selected shows from the two pop-up menus, as shown in Figure 2-10. If you want to also include individual episodes or episodes on playlists, select the appropriate check boxes in the Shows, Episodes, and Include Episodes from Playlists sections of the TV Shows pane.

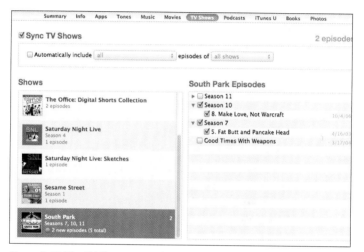

Figure 2-10: The TV Shows pane determines how TV shows are synced with your iPhone.

Podcasts, iTunes U, and books

You can also sync podcasts, educational content from iTunes U, two types of books — e-books for reading and audiobooks for listening — and photos.

Podcasts

To transfer podcasts to your iPhone, select the Sync Podcasts check box in the Podcasts pane. Then you can automatically include however many podcasts you want by making selections from the two pop-up menus, as shown in Figure 2-11. If you have podcast episodes on playlists, you can include them by selecting the appropriate check box in the Include Episodes from Playlists section.

Figure 2-11: The Podcasts pane determines which podcasts are copied to your iPhone.

To watch (or listen) to podcasts, you need the free Podcasts app from the App Store. For more information on apps and the App Store, read Chapter 9.

iTunes U

To sync educational content from iTunes U, first select the Sync iTunes U check box to enable iTunes U syncing. Then choose how many episodes to include and whether you want all collections or only selected collections from the two pop-up menus. If you want to also include individual items or items on playlists, select the appropriate check boxes in the Items section and Include Items from Playlists section of the iTunes U pane.

To enjoy iTunes U content, you need the free iTunes U app from the App Store.

Books

By now we're sure you know the drill: You can sync all your e-books or audiobooks or just sync selected titles by choosing the appropriate buttons and check boxes in the Books pane.

To read e-books, you need the free iBooks app from the App Store.

Photos

Syncing photos is a little different from syncing other media because your iPhone has a built-in camera — two cameras, actually — and you may want to copy pictures or videos you take with the iPhone to your computer, as well as copy pictures stored on your computer to your iPhone.

The iPhone syncs photos and videos, too, with the following programs:

 ✔ **Mac:** Aperture version 3.2 or later or iPhoto version 9.2 or later

 ✔ **PC:** Adobe Photoshop Elements or Adobe Photoshop Album

 If you're a Dropbox user on your Mac or PC, you can choose to copy your photos and videos to a special folder named Camera Uploads within your Dropbox folder. Dropbox prompts you for confirmation before copying any items.

You can also sync photos with any folder on your computer that contains images.

In the Photos pane, select the Sync Photos From check box, and then choose an application or folder from the pop-up menu (which says iPhoto in Figure 2-12).

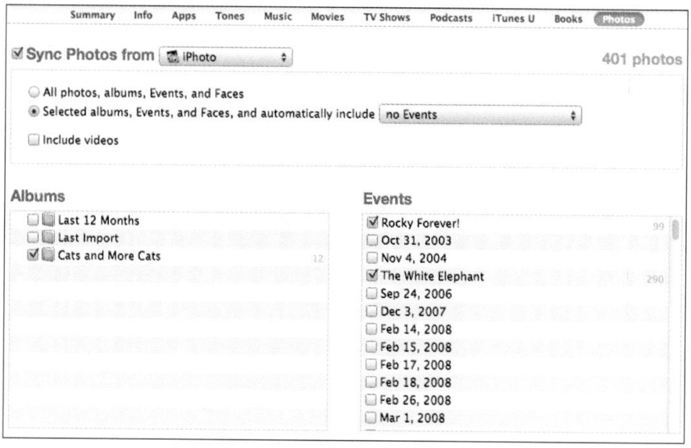

| Summary | Info | Apps | Tones | Music | Movies | TV Shows | Podcasts | iTunes U | Books | Photos |

☑ Sync Photos from [🖼 iPhoto ‡]   401 photos

    ○ All photos, albums, Events, and Faces
    ◉ Selected albums, Events, and Faces, and automatically include [no Events ‡]
    ☐ Include videos

Albums
- ☐ 🖼 Last 12 Months
- ☐ 🖼 Last Import
- ☑ 🖼 Cats and More Cats   12

Events
- ☑ Rocky Forever!   99
- ☐ Oct 31, 2003
- ☐ Nov 4, 2004
- ☑ The White Elephant   290
- ☐ Sep 24, 2006
- ☐ Dec 3, 2007
- ☐ Feb 14, 2008
- ☐ Feb 15, 2008
- ☐ Feb 17, 2008
- ☐ Feb 18, 2008
- ☐ Feb 26, 2008
- ☐ Mar 1, 2008

Figure 2-12: The Photos pane determines which photos will be synchronized with your iPhone.

If you choose an application that supports photo albums (such as Photoshop Elements, Aperture, or iPhoto), projects (Aperture), events (iPhoto), facial recognition (Aperture or iPhoto), or any combination thereof, you can automatically include recent projects (Aperture), events (iPhoto), or faces (Aperture and iPhoto) by making a selection from the same pop-up menu (refer to Figure 2-12).

If you're using iPhoto, you can also type a word or phrase in the search field (an oval with a magnifying glass) to search for a specific event or events.

If you choose a folder full of images, you can create subfolders inside it that will appear as albums on your iPhone. But if you choose an application that doesn't support albums or events, or a single folder full of images with no subfolders, you have to transfer all or nothing.

Because we selected iPhoto in the Sync Photos From menu, and iPhoto supports projects and faces in addition to albums and photos, we have the option of syncing any combination of photos, projects, albums, and faces.

If you've taken any photos with your iPhone or saved images from a web page, an e-mail, an MMS message, or an iMessage since the last time you synced, the appropriate program launches (or the appropriate folder is selected), and you have the option of downloading the pictures to your computer.

3

Making Calls and Sending Messages

In This Chapter

▶ Making a call

▶ Visualizing visual voicemail

▶ Recording a greeting

▶ Dialing by voice

▶ Receiving a call

▶ Sending and receiving SMS, MMS, and iMessage messages

▶ Video chatting with FaceTime

*A*side from making it easy for you to make regular phone calls, sending text messages is also simple and fun with the iPhone. This chapter is devoted to the nifty ways you can handle wireless calls on an iPhone and keep in touch with text messages. We focus on the three types of iPhone message protocols: SMS, MMS, and iMessage.

Making a Call

To make a call, start by tapping the Phone icon on the Home screen. You can then make calls by tapping any of the icons that show up at the bottom of the screen: Favorites, Recents, Contacts, Keypad, or Voicemail. And the 3GS and iPhone 4 offer one additional way to call — you can dial a phone number or a particular person by voice. If you have an iPhone 4S or iPhone 5, you can also use Siri, the voice assistant, which we cover in Chapter 4. Let's take these options one by one.

Contacts

You can get your snail-mail addresses, e-mail addresses, and (most relevant for this chapter) phone numbers that reside on your PC or Mac into the iPhone by syncing or via iCloud (see Chapter 2 if you need help with this task). Assuming that you've already mastered that task, all those addresses and phone numbers are now hanging out in one place. Tap the Contacts icon inside the Phone application or the Contacts icon within the Utilities folder (by default, found on the second screen page). Here's how to make those contacts work for you:

1. **Inside the Phone application, tap Contacts.**

2. **Flick your finger so the list of contacts on the screen scrolls rapidly up or down.**

   You can also move your finger along the alphabet on the right edge of the Contacts list or tap a tiny letter to jump to names beginning with that letter.

   You also can find a list of potential matches by starting to type the name of a contact in the search field near the top of the list. Or you can type the name of the place your contact works. You may have to flick to get the search field into view. You can also find people by using Spotlight search (see Chapter 1).

3. **When you're at or near the appropriate contact name, stop the scrolling by tapping the screen.**

   Note that when you tap to stop the scrolling, that tap doesn't select an item in the list. That may seem counterintuitive the first few times you try it.

   Double-tap the status bar (which reads All Contacts) to automatically scroll to the top of the list. This is useful if you're really popular and have a whole bunch of names among your contacts.

4. **Tap the name of the person you want to call (see Figure 3-1).**

   You see a number of fields with the person's phone numbers, physical and e-mail addresses, and possibly even a mug shot. Odds are pretty good that the person has more than one phone number, so the hardest decision you must make is choosing which of these to call.

5. **Tap the phone number, and the iPhone initiates the call.**

If you lumped your contacts into Groups on your computer, reflecting, say, different departments in your company or friends from work, friends from school, and so on, you can tap the Groups button on the upper-left side of the All Contacts screen to access these groups.

Figure 3-1: You get this contact absolutely free!

 Your own iPhone phone number, lest you forget it, appears at the top of the Contacts list, if you arrived in Contacts from the Phone application.

Favorites

Consider Favorites the iPhone equivalent of speed-dialing. It's where you can keep a list of the people and numbers you dial most often. Merely tap the person's name in Favorites to call that person.

 You can set up as many favorites as you need for a person. For example, you can create separate Favorites listings for your spouse's office phone number, FaceTime number, and cell number.

Setting up Favorites is a breeze. When looking at one of your contacts, you may have noticed the Add to Favorites button. When you tap this button, all the phone numbers you have for that person pop up. Tap the number you want to make into a favorite, and it turns up on the list.

To rearrange the order in which your favorites are displayed, tap Edit; then, to the right of the person you want to move, press your finger against the symbol that looks like three short horizontal lines stacked on top of one another. Drag that symbol to the place on the list where you want your favorite contact to appear.

You can designate new favorites from within the Favorites screen by tapping the + symbol at the upper-right corner of the screen. Doing so brings you back to Contacts. From there, choose the appropriate person and number. A star appears next to any contact's number picked as a favorite.

If any of your chosen folks happen to fall out of favor, you can easily kick them off the Favorites roster. Here's how:

1. **Tap the Edit button in the upper-left corner of the screen.**

   A red circle with a horizontal white line appears to the left of each name in the list.

2. **Tap the circle next to the A-lister getting the heave-ho.**

   The horizontal white line is now vertical, and a red Delete button appears to the right of the name, as shown in Figure 3-2.

3. **Tap Delete.**

   The person (or one of his or her given phone numbers) is no longer afforded the privilege of being in your iPhone inner circle.

Booting someone off the Favorites list does not remove that person from the main Contacts list.

Figure 3-2: No offense, just a demonstration.

Recents

Tapping the Recents icon displays the iPhone call log. The Recents feature houses logs of all recent calls made or received, as well as calls that you missed. Tap All to show all the recent calls and Missed to show just those you missed. Under the All list, completed calls and missed calls that have been returned by clicking the red entry are shown in black; missed calls that haven't been returned in this fashion are shown in red. You also see a descriptor for the phone you were calling or from which you received a call (home, mobile, and so on).

By tapping the small blue circle with the right-pointing arrow next to an item in the list, you can access information about the time a call was made or missed, as well as any known information about the caller from your Contacts information. To return a call, just tap anywhere on the name.

If one of the calls you missed came from someone who isn't already in your Contacts, you can add him or her. Tap the right-pointing arrow, and then tap the Create New Contact button. If the person is among your Contacts but has a new number, tap the Add to Existing Contact button. When the list gets too long, tap Edit and then tap Clear to clean it up.

Keypad

From time to time, of course, you have to dial the number of a person or company who hasn't earned a spot in your Contacts.

That's when you want to tap the keypad icon to bring up the large keys on the virtual touch-tone keypad you see in Figure 3-3. It's surprisingly simple to manually dial a number on this keypad. Just tap the appropriate keys and tap Call.

Figure 3-3: A virtually familiar way to dial.

To add this number to your Contacts list, tap the + key on the keypad (it's the one with the silhouette of a person next to it) and click either Create New Contact or Add to Existing Contact.

Dialing with your voice

If you have an iPhone 3GS or 4, you can make a call by simply opening your mouth, using Voice Control. Owners of the iPhone 4S and iPhone 5 can call using *Siri*, the iPhone voice assistant. Read more about both of these great features in Chapter 4.

Visual voicemail

How often have you had to listen to four or five voicemail messages before getting to the message you want to hear? As shown in Figure 3-4, the iPhone's clever visual voicemail presents a list of your voicemail messages in the order received. But you need not listen to those messages in that order.

How do you even know you have voicemail?

- ✔ A red circle showing the number of pending messages awaiting your attention appears above the Phone icon on the Home screen or above the Voicemail icon from within the Phone application.

- ✔ You may also see a notification on the iPhone display that says something like, "New voicemail from Ed." You can configure these notifications from the Notifications item within the Settings app.

Whatever draws you in, tap the Voicemail icon to display the list of voicemail messages. You see the caller's phone number, assuming this info is known through CallerID, and in some cases his or her name. Or you see the word *Unknown.*

Play head Scrubber bar

Figure 3-4: Visual voicemail in action.

The beauty of all this, of course, is that you can ignore (or at least put off listening to) certain messages.

A blue dot next to a name or number signifies that you haven't heard the message yet.

To play back a voicemail, tap the name or number in question. Then tap the tiny Play/Pause button that shows up to the left. Tap once more to pause the message; tap again to resume. Tap the Speaker button if you want to hear the message through the iPhone's speakerphone.

Tap the blue arrow next to a caller's name or number to bring up any contact info on the person or to add the caller to your Contacts.

The tiny playhead along the Scrubber bar (refer to Figure 3-4) shows you the length of the message and how much of the message you've heard. If you hate when callers ramble on forever, you can drag the playhead to rapidly advance through a message. Perhaps more importantly, if you miss something, you can replay that segment.

Returning a call is as simple as tapping the green Call Back button. And you can delete a voicemail by tapping Delete.

If you have no phone service, you'll see a message that says *Visual Voicemail is currently unavailable*.

You can listen to your iPhone voicemail from another phone. Just dial your iPhone number and, while the greeting plays, enter your voicemail password. You can set up such a password by tapping Settings from the Home screen and then tapping Phone. Tap Change Voicemail Password. You're asked to enter your current voicemail password if you already have one. Type it and tap Done. If you haven't set up a password previously, tap Done. You're asked to type a new password; then you tap Done twice.

Recording a greeting

You have two choices when it comes to your voicemail greeting. You can accept a generic greeting with your phone number by default. Or you can create a custom greeting in your own voice by following these steps:

1. **Inside the voicemail application, tap the Greeting button.**

2. **Tap Custom.**

3. **Tap Record and start dictating a clever, deserving-of-being-on-the-iPhone voicemail greeting.**

4. **When you have finished recording, tap Stop.**

5. **Review the greeting by pressing Play.**

6. **If the greeting is worthy, tap Save. If not, tap Cancel and start over at Step 1.**

Receiving a Call

It's wonderful to have numerous options for making a call. But what are your choices when somebody calls you? The answer depends on whether you are willing to take the call. Luckily, the iPhone includes caller ID display for those numbers in your Contacts list.

Accepting the call

To accept a call, you have several options:

- Tap Answer and greet the caller in whatever language makes sense.

- If the phone is locked, drag the slider to the right.

- Swipe up and tap the Reply with Message to send a text message or iMessage to the caller.

- Swipe up and tap the Remind Me Later to display a reminder to call the person back.

- If you are donning the stereo earbuds that come with the iPhone, click the microphone button.

If you are listening to music in your iPhone's iPod when a call comes in, the song stops playing and you have to decide whether to take the call. If you do, the music resumes from where you left off when the conversation ends.

Rejecting the call

We're going to assume that you're not a cold-hearted person out to break a caller's heart. Rather, we assume that you are a busy person who will call back at a more convenient time. Keeping that positive spin in mind, here are three ways to reject a call on the spot and send the call to voicemail:

- ✓ Tap Decline. Couldn't be easier than that.

- ✓ Press the Sleep/Wake button twice in rapid succession. (The button is on the top of the device.)

- ✓ Using the supplied headset, press and hold the Microphone button for a couple of seconds and then let go. Two beeps let you know that the call was indeed rejected.

Sometimes you're perfectly willing to take a call but you need to silence the ringer or turn off the vibration. To do so, press the Sleep/Wake button a single time, or press one of the volume buttons. You'll still have the opportunity to answer.

iOS 6 introduces *Do Not Disturb*, which you can configure within Settings⇨Notifications. When you turn on Do Not Disturb within Settings, all alerts, vibration, and ringtones are turned off, and you see a moon icon in the status bar. (You can also specify just a handful of contacts that can reach you no matter what.)

While on a Call

You can do lots of things while talking on an iPhone, such as consulting your calendar, taking notes, or checking the weather. Press the Home button to get to the apps that let you perform these tasks.

If you're using Wi-Fi or 3G/4G and are on an AT&T iPhone, you can also surf the web (through Safari) while talking on the phone. But you can't surf while you talk if your only outlet to cyberspace is the AT&T EDGE network or a CDMA network such as the ones that Sprint and Verizon rely on.

Here are other things you can do while on a call:

- ✓ **Mute a call:** From the main call screen (shown in Figure 3-5), tap Mute. Now you need not mutter under your breath when the caller ticks you off. Tap Mute again to unmute the sound.

Figure 3-5: Managing calls.

- ✓ **Tap Contacts to display the Contacts list:** This option is useful if you want to look up a friend's number while you're talking to another pal or you want to add someone to a conference call.

- ✓ **Place a call on hold:** This option depends on the phone you're using. If you're on an iPhone 4/4S or 5, touch and hold the aforementioned Mute button. On older devices, just tap Hold. Tap Hold (or Mute) again to take the person off hold. You might put a caller on hold to answer another incoming call or to make a second call yourself. The next section shows you how to deal with more than one call at a time.

- ✓ **Tap Keypad to bring back the keypad:** This feature is useful if you have to type touchtones to access another voicemail system or respond to an automated menu system.

✔ **Use the speakerphone:** Tap Speaker to listen to a call through the iPhone's internal speakers without having to hold the device up to your mouth. If you've paired the iPhone with a Bluetooth device, the control is labeled Audio Source instead, as shown in Figure 3-6. Tap Audio Source and then tap Speaker (if you want the speakerphone), iPhone (if you want to hold up the phone to your ear), or the name of the Bluetooth device. A tiny speaker icon appears next to your selection, as shown in Figure 3-7.

✔ **Make a conference call:** With one caller on the line, tap the Mute button on an iPhone 4/4S or 5 (or tap Hold on an older phone) to put the person on hold. Tap Add Call, and the keypad appears so that you can enter another phone number. When the second person is on the line, tap the Merge Calls button that now appears on the screen. All three of you are now connected.

Figure 3-6: Tap Audio Source to change how you are taking the call.

Figure 3-7: The speakerphone is active.

FaceTime: Seeing Is Believing

Using FaceTime is as easy as making a regular call on the iPhone, but you get to actually *see* the person on the other end of the line. We think a lot of people will want to see you: an old college roommate living halfway around the world; grandparents living miles away; or an old flame in a distant location.

Fortunately, FaceTime comes with at least two major benefits *besides* the video:

- ✔ FaceTime calls don't count against your regular plan minutes.

- ✔ The audio quality on FaceTime calls is superior to a regular cell phone connection.

But FaceTime also has a couple of major caveats:

- ✔ Both you and the party you're talking to must have an iPhone 4/4S or 5, a second or third-generation iPad, a Mac computer running OS X Lion or Mountain Lion, or a recent iPod touch. (Okay, so maybe that's not much of a caveat after all.) Apple is pushing to make FaceTime a video standard that the entire tech industry can embrace, allowing you to someday (and maybe even by the time you read this) make FaceTime calls from iPhones and other Apple devices to other handsets and computers that don't carry an Apple logo. We'll see.

- ✔ Both you and the caller at the other end have to access either Wi-Fi or a cellular network. The quality of the experience depends on a solid connection.

If you meet the requirements, here's how to make FaceTime happen:

1. **The first time you make a FaceTime call to another iPhone, dial the person's regular iPhone number as usual, using any of the methods we describe in this chapter.**

   You use an e-mail address instead if you're using FaceTime to call an iPod touch, an iPad, or a Mac.

2. **After a regular call is established and you've broached the subject of going video, you can tap the FaceTime button shown in Figure 3-8.**

   A few seconds later, the other person gets the option to Decline or Accept the FaceTime invitation by tapping the red button or the green button, respectively, as shown in Figure 3-9. If the answer is Accept, you need to wait a few seconds before you can see the other person.

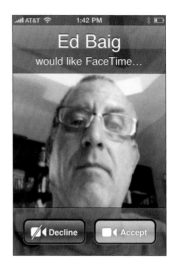

Figure 3-8: Tap FaceTime to literally watch what happens.

Figure 3-9: Say "yes" to see me.

You can also use the Siri voice assistant (discussed in greater detail in Chapter 4) to make a FaceTime call. Just ask Siri to "FaceTime with Dad" or whomever else you'd want to engage in a video call, and she'll make the proper arrangements.

When someone requests FaceTime with you, you'll appreciate being able to politely decline a FaceTime call. Cool as it can be to see and be seen, ask yourself if you really want to be seen, say, when you just got out of bed.

Although your initial FaceTime call often involves AT&T, Verizon, Sprint, or C Spire, FaceTime also works over a Wi-Fi connection. Search for any FaceTime calls you previously made by tapping an entry for that call in Recents. The iPhone knows to take the call straight to video, though of course the person you're talking to has to accept the invitation each time.

You can do FaceTime also by tapping a pal's listings in Contacts.

So what is a FaceTime call like? In our experience, first-time reactions were gleeful. Not only are you seeing the other person, but the quality of the video is also typically good. You also see your own mug in a small picture-in-picture (PiP) window (as shown in Figure 3-10), which you can drag to a corner of the screen. The PiP image represents what the other person sees, so it's a good way of knowing, short of the other person telling you, if your face has dropped out of the frame.

Recipient sees this PiP

Mute audio   End call   Switch cameras

Figure 3-10: Bob can see Ed and Ed can see Bob.

 You can use FaceTime in portrait or landscape mode. You might find it easier to bring another person into a scene in landscape mode.

 Apple says the front camera has been fine-tuned for FaceTime usage, which in photography-speak means the camera has the proper field of view and focal length. But at times, you'll want to employ the iPhone's main camera on the rear to best show off your surroundings and give the caller an idea of where you are.

To toggle between the front and main cameras, tap the icon at the bottom-right corner of the screen (refer to Figure 3-10).

If you want to mute a FaceTime video call, tap the microphone icon with the slash running through it. The caller can continue to see you but not hear you.

Unfortunately, you can't go from FaceTime to an audio-only call without hanging up and redialing. Similarly, if you drop a FaceTime call because of a Wi-Fi/cellular hiccup or some other problem, you have to redial via FaceTime or your provider, depending on whether you want the call to be video or only audio.

To block all FaceTime calls, tap Settings from the Home screen, tap FaceTime, and make sure FaceTime is off. If you can't find the FaceTime button or wonder why you're not getting FaceTime calls, go back into Settings and make sure this option is turned on. Although you are in FaceTime Settings, you'll notice that you can list one or more e-mail addresses by which a caller can reach you for a video call, along with your iPhone's phone number.

If you want to momentarily check out another iPhone app while on a FaceTime call, press the Home button and then tap the icon for the app you have in mind. At this point, you can still talk over FaceTime, but you'll no longer see the person. Tap the green bar at the top of the screen to bring the person back in front of you.

Messaging

The Messages application lets you exchange short text messages with any cell phone that supports the SMS protocol. Your iPhone also supports the MMS protocol, which lets you exchange pictures, contacts, videos, ringtones (and other audio recordings) with any cell phone that supports the MMS protocol. Finally, if you're using any iPhone that's running iOS 5 or 6, you can send iMessages with text, video, or audio — free of charge — to any other iOS 5 or 6 device. That list includes another iPhone, an iPad, or an iPod touch, as well as a Mac running OSX Lion or Mountain Lion.

MMS support is built into iPhone OS 3.0 and higher and works with all iPhone models except for the first generation iPhone.

Typing text on a cell phone with a 12-key numeric keypad is an unnatural act, which is why many cell phone users have never sent a single SMS or MMS message. The iPhone changes that. The intelligent virtual keyboard makes it easy to compose short text messages, and the big, bright, high-resolution screen makes it a pleasure to read them. (You can even command Siri to create a text message for you using only your voice!)

Before we get to the part where you send or receive a message, however, let's go over some SMS/MMS basics:

- **Both sender and receiver must have SMS- or MMS-enabled mobile phones.** Your iPhone qualifies, as does almost any mobile phone made in the past few years and iPads and iPod touches with iOS 5 or higher. Keep in mind that if you send messages to folks with phones that don't support SMS or MMS — or to folks who choose not to pay extra for messaging services — they will never get your message, nor will they know you sent a message.

- **Some phones (not the iPhone, of course) limit SMS messages to 160 characters.** If you try to send a longer message to one of these phones, your message may be cut off or split into multiple shorter messages. The point is that it's a good idea to keep SMS messages brief.

- **You can send or receive messages only over your wireless carrier's network (AT&T, Sprint, or Verizon in the U.S.).** In other words, SMS and MMS messages can't be sent or received over a Wi-Fi connection — however, iMessage (which we discuss in a page or two) works fine over both Wi-Fi and cellular connections.

- **Regardless of which carrier you choose, you'll encounter a bewildering array of pricing options.** In the United States, AT&T and Verizon data plans do not include SMS or MMS messages. Verizon and Sprint offer packages with a 200- or 250-message limit starting at around $5 per month; AT&T offers only unlimited messages starting at $20 per month. If you don't subscribe to a messaging plan from your wireless operator, you'll pay 20¢ or 30¢ per message sent or received.

Each individual message in a conversation counts against this total, even if it's only a one-word reply such as "OK," or "CUL8R" (which is Teenager for "see you later").

Okay, now that we have that out of the way, let's start with how to send messages.

Sending an SMS message

 Tap the Messages icon on the Home screen to launch the Messages application (known as Text on earlier versions of the iPhone software), and then tap the little pencil-and-paper icon in the top-right corner of the screen to start a new text message.

The To field is active and awaiting your input. You can do three things at this point:

- ✓ If the recipient isn't in your Contacts list, type his or her cell phone number.

- ✓ If the recipient *is* in your Contacts list, type the first few letters of the name. A list of matching contacts appears. Scroll through it if necessary and tap the name of the contact.

  The more letters you type, the shorter the list becomes.

- ✓ Tap the blue plus (+) icon on the right side of the To field to select a name from your Contacts list.

There's a fourth option if you want to compose the message first and address it later. Tap inside the text-entry field (the oval-shaped area just above the keyboard and to the left of the Send button) to activate it and then type your message. When you're finished typing, tap the To field and use one of the preceding techniques to address your message.

When you have finished addressing and composing, tap the Send button to send your message on its merry way. That's all there is to it.

Receiving an SMS message

First things first. If you want an alert to sound when you receive a message, tap the Settings icon on your Home screen, tap Sounds, tap the Text Tone item, and then tap one of the available sounds. You can audition the sounds by tapping them.

You hear the sounds when you audition them in the Settings app, even if you have the Ring/Silent switch set to Silent. After you exit the Settings application, however, you *won't* hear a sound when a message arrives if the Ring/Silent switch is set to Silent, or if you've turned on the Do Not Disturb feature. Your iPhone still displays a notification, however.

If you *don't* want to hear an alert when a message arrives, instead of tapping one of the listed sounds, tap the first item in the list: None.

If you receive a message when your phone is asleep, all or part of the text message and the name of the sender appear on the Unlock screen when you wake your phone.

If your phone is awake and unlocked when a message arrives, all or part of the message and the name of the sender appear at the top of the screen (as well as in the Notification Center, which you can display by swiping downward from the top of the screen). At the same time, the Messages icon on the Home screen displays the number of unread messages (see Figure 3-11).

You can, however, set your iPhone to display an alert (which enables you to reply immediately). Tap Settings and tap Notifications, and then tap the Messages entry and choose the Alerts setting. Now you can read or reply to the message by tapping Reply.

If you're not using alerts, tap the Messages icon to read or reply to a message. If a message other than the one you're interested in appears on the screen when you launch the Messages application, tap Messages in the top-left corner of the screen and then tap the recipient's name; that person's messages appear on the screen.

Figure 3-11: What you see if your iPhone is set to alert notification when a message arrives.

To reply to the message on the screen, tap the text-entry field to the left of the Send button, and the keyboard appears. Type your reply and then tap Send.

Tap the Dictation key — the key to the left of Space, which bears a microphone symbol — and you can dictate text directly into the text-entry field!

Your conversation is saved as a series of text bubbles. Your messages appear on the right side of the screen in green bubbles (for MMS/SMS) or blue bubbles (for iMessages); the other person's messages appear on the left in gray bubbles, as shown in Figure 3-12.

You can delete a conversation in two ways:

✓ **If you're viewing the conversation:** Tap the Edit button at the top right of the conversation screen. A circle appears to the left of each text bubble. Tap a text bubble and a red check mark appears in the circle. When you've added a red check mark to all the text bubbles you want to delete, tap the red Delete button at the bottom-left of the screen. Or, to delete the entire conversation in one fell swoop, tap the Clear All button in the top-left corner of the screen.

✔ **If you're viewing the list of text messages:** Tap the Edit button at the top left of the Text Messages list, tap the red minus icon that appears to the left of the person's name, and then tap the Delete button that appears to the right of the name.

Figure 3-12: This is what an SMS conversation looks like.

MMS: Like SMS with media

To send a picture or video (iPhone 3GS, 4/4S, and 5 only) in a message, follow the instructions for sending a text message and then tap the camera icon to the left of the text-entry field at the bottom of the screen. You then have the option of using an existing picture or video or taking a new one. You can also add text to photos or videos if you like. When you're finished, tap the Send button.

If you *receive* a picture or video in a message, it appears in a bubble just like text. Tap it to see it full-screen.

Tap the icon in the lower-left corner (the one that looks like an arrow trying to escape from a rectangle) for additional options. If you don't see the icon, tap the picture or video once and the icon magically appears.

iMessage: iOS 5/iOS 6 messaging

Although the party is limited to owners of iOS 5 and iOS 6 devices (at the time of this writing), iMessage provides everything that MMS includes — video, locations, contacts, and photos — and iMessages can be sent over a Wi-Fi connection as well as a cellular connection. Plus, they're as free as the air around you!

iMessage operates just like MMS. To verify that you're using iMessage, check the information line at the top of a conversation — it should read *iMessage*. (Again, your conversation bubbles also appear in blue if you're sending iMessages.)

4

Taking the iPhone Siri-ously

*H*ow could you not love Siri? The intelligent voice-activated virtual personal assistant living like a genie inside the iPhone 4S and iPhone 5 not only *hear*s what you have to say but attempts to figure out the intent of your words. Siri then does her best to respond to your wishes. She — yes, it's a female voice, at least at the time of this writing — can help you dictate and send a message, get directions, call a friend, arrange a wake-up call, search the web, find a decent place to eat, and lots more. Siri talks back, too, sometimes with humor and other times with attitude. Siri doesn't work on older iPhones, only on the 4S and 5.

Apple concedes that Siri isn't perfect — the feature still carries that "not quite finished" beta tag. In our experience, Siri sometimes mishears and sometimes doesn't quite know what we had in mind. But blemishes and all, we think she's pretty special. We think you'll agree.

Summoning Siri

When you first set up the iPhone 4S or iPhone 5, you have the option of turning on Siri. If you did so, you're good to go. If you didn't, tap Settings⇨General⇨Siri and flip the switch so that On is showing. (If you do turn Siri off on the 4S or 5, it effectively turns Voice Control on.)

To call Siri into action, press and hold the Home button until you hear a tone and then start talking. Pretty simple, eh? At the bottom of the screen, you see a picture of a microphone inside a circle, as shown in Figure 4-1. The question, "What can I help you with?" appears on the screen. Alternatively, when the screen isn't locked, bring the phone up to your ear and wait for that same tone, and then talk. (This feature is called *Raise to Speak*, and you can turn it on from the same Siri screen in Settings.)

Siri also responds when you press a button on a Bluetooth headset.

Tap here to see
sample Siri queries

Figure 4-1: Siri is eager to respond.

What happens next is up to you. You can ask a wide range of questions or issue voice commands. If you didn't get your words out fast enough or Siri misunderstood you, tap the microphone icon and try again.

Siri relies on voice recognition and artificial intelligence. She responds in a conversational (if still slightly robotic) manner. But using Siri isn't entirely a hands-free experience. Spoken words are supplemented by information on the iPhone screen (as you see in the next section).

Where does Siri get that information? She seeks answers from the web using sources such as Yelp and WolframAlpha. She taps into Location Services on the phone. And Siri works with numerous apps on the 4S/5: Phone, Mail, Safari, Music, Messages, Calendar, Reminders, Maps, Weather, Stocks, Notes, Clock, and Contacts. If you're running iOS 6, you can also run third-party apps with Siri (try saying "Run" followed by the name of the app).

Indeed, from your contacts, Siri might be able to determine who your spouse, coworkers, and friends are, as well as knowing where you live. You might ask, "How do I get home from here?" and Siri fires up Maps to help you on your way. Or you can ask, "Find a good Italian restaurant near Barbara's house," and Siri serves up a list, sorted by Yelp rating.

Siri requires Internet access, either via Wi-Fi or your cellular provider. A lot of factors go into its accuracy, including surrounding noises and unfamiliar accents.

Figuring out what to ask

The beauty of Siri is that there's no designated protocol you must follow when talking to her. Asking, "Will I need an umbrella tomorrow?", as shown in Figure 4-2, produces the same result as "What is the weather forecast around here?"

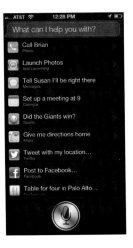

Figure 4-2: Siri can help you prepare for the weather.

Figure 4-3: Siri can help out in many ways.

If you're not sure what to ask, tap the circled *i* to list sample questions or commands, as shown in Figure 4-3. You can actually tap on any of these examples to see even more samples.

Here are some of the ways Siri can lend a hand, um, voice:

- **Phone:** "Call my wife on her cell phone."
- **Music:** "Play Frank Sinatra."
- **Messages:** "Send a message to Nancy to reschedule lunch."
- **Calendar:** "Set up a meeting for 9 a.m. to discuss funding."
- **Reminders:** "Remind me to take my medicine at 8 a.m. tomorrow."
- **Maps:** "Find an ATM near here."
- **Mail:** "Mail the tenant about the recent check."
- **Stocks:** "What is the Dow at?"
- **Web search:** "Who was the 19th president of the United States?"

> ✓ **Movies:** "When is *The Hobbit* showing?"
>
> ✓ **WolframAlpha:** "How many calories are in a blueberry muffin?"
>
> ✓ **Sports:** "What's the score in the Cardinals game?"
>
> ✓ **Clock:** "Wake me up at 8:30 in the morning."

Voice isn't the solution to everything. Putting Siri to work typically involves a combination of using voice, touch, and your eyes to see what's on the screen.

Using dictation

In many instances where you'd otherwise use the iPhone touchscreen keyboard, you can now use the iOS Dictation feature instead. In lieu of typing, tap the microphone icon on the keyboard and speak. Tap Done when you're done. Dictation works as you search the web, take notes, compose messages, and so on. You can even update your Facebook status by voice.

Correcting mistakes

As we've pointed out, as good as Siri is, she sometimes needs to be put in her place. Fortunately, you can correct her mistakes fairly easily. The simplest way is to tap the microphone icon and try your query again. You can say something along the lines of, "I meant Botswana."

You can also tap the bubble showing what Siri thinks you said, and make edits by using the touch keyboard or by voice. If a word is underlined in blue, you can use the keyboard or your voice to make a correction.

Before Siri sends a dictated message, she seeks your permission first. That's a safeguard you'll come to appreciate. If you need to modify the message, you can do so by saying such things as, "Change Tuesday to Wednesday" or "Add: I'm excited to see you, exclamation mark" — indeed, *I'm excited to see you* and *!* will be added.

Settings to make Siri smarter

From the Siri screen in Settings, you can tell Siri which language you want to converse in. Out of the gate, Siri was available in English (United States, United Kingdom, or Australian), French, and German.

You can also request voice feedback from Siri all the time, or just when you're using a hands-free headset.

In the My Info field in Settings, you can tell Siri who you are. When you tap My Info, your Contacts list appears. Tap your own name in Contacts.

If you're concerned about Siri intruding when you raise the phone to your ear to make a call, head to Settings as well to turn the Raise to Speak feature off.

As noted, you can call upon Siri even from the Lock screen. That's the default setting anyway. Consider this feature a mixed blessing. Not having to type a passcode to get Siri to do her thing is convenient. On the other hand, if your phone ends up with the wrong person, he or she would be able to use Siri to make a call, send an e-mail, or send a message in your name, bypassing whatever passcode security you thought was in place. We suspect Apple will close this loophole, perhaps even by the time you read this. But if they don't get around to it and you find this potential scenario scary, tap Settings➪General➪Passcode Lock. Then enter your passcode and switch the Siri option under Passcode Lock from On to Off.

Voice dialing

Several cell phones of recent vintage let you dial a name or number by voice. Bark out "Call Mom" or "Dial 212-555-1212," and such handsets oblige. Your engaging virtual personal assistant, Siri, can do that too.

But you can take advantage of voice calling (and some other functions too) with an older iPhone that doesn't have Siri. It's all part of a feature called Voice Control.

If you have an iPhone that predates the 4S, you have two ways to summon the Voice Control feature:

✒ Press and hold the Home button until the Voice Control screen shown in Figure 4-4 appears. The screen displays wavy lines that move as you speak. Scrolling in the background are some of the commands you can say out loud ("Play Artist," "Previous Track," and so on). Don't blurt out anything until you hear a quick double-beep. The iPhone repeats the command it thinks it heard.

✒ Press and hold the center button on the wired headset. Once again, wait for an audible cue and then tell the iPhone what you have in mind.

Figure 4-4: Tell the iPhone to dial the phone or play a song.

Voice Control works quite nicely with the wired headset included with your iPhone. It works also with some Bluetooth headsets and car kits. If you use a wireless headset that's not supported, you have to hold the phone up to your lips if you want it to respond to voice commands.

You definitely want to wait for voice confirmation after you've spoken. In our experience, Voice Control isn't perfect, especially in a noisy environment. So if you're dialing a name or number, make sure the iPhone is indeed calling the person you had in mind. There's no telling what kind of trouble you might get into otherwise.

Wait for the tone and speak clearly, especially if you're in a noisy environment. You can dial by number, as in "Dial 202-555-1212." You can dial a name, as in "Call Bob LeVitus" or "Dial Ed Baig." Or you can be a tad more specific, as in "Dial Bob LeVitus mobile" or "Call Ed Baig home." Before actually dialing the phone, an automated female voice repeats what she thinks she heard.

If the person you're calling has multiple phone numbers and you fail to specify which one, the female voice prompts you, "Ed Baig, home, mobile, or work?" Tell her which one it is, or say "Cancel" if you decide not to call.

When the Voice Control screen appears, let go of the Home button before speaking a command. Otherwise, your thumb may cover the microphone, making it more difficult for the iPhone to understand your intent.

Voice Control need not be in Americanized English. From the Home screen, tap Settings, General, International, Voice Control. Then choose from nearly two dozen language options in the list. Choices include Australian English and English as spoken in the U.K., and versions of Chinese customized for Cantonese, China, and Taiwan.

5

Playing Music and Videos

In This Chapter

▶ Using the built-in iPod

▶ Managing your tunes

▶ Finding videos to watch

*B*esides being a super-cool phone, your iPhone is also one heck of an iPod. In this chapter, we show you how to use your iPhone to play both audio and video.

We assume that you already synced your iPhone with your computer or with iCloud and that your iPhone contains audio content (songs or audiobooks). You should also be running the latest version of iTunes on your Mac or PC.

Are you ready to rock?

Using the iPod in Your iPhone

To use your iPhone as an iPod, tap the Music icon in the bottom-right corner of the Home screen. At the bottom of the screen, you should see five icons: Playlists, Artists, Songs, Albums, and More. If you don't see these icons, tap the Back button in the top-left corner of the screen (the one that looks like a little arrow pointing to the left).

Or, if you're holding your iPhone sideways (the long edges parallel to the ground), rotate it 90 degrees so that it's upright (the short edges parallel to the ground).

Playlists

Tap the Playlists icon at the bottom of the screen and a list of playlists appears. If you don't have any playlists on your iPhone, don't sweat it. Just know that if you had some, this is where they'd be. (*Playlists* let you organize songs around a particular theme or mood: opera arias, romantic ballads, British Invasion, whatever.)

Tap a playlist, and you see a list of the songs it contains. If the list is longer than one screen, flick upwards to scroll down. Tap a song in the list and it plays — when the song is over, your iPhone continues with the next song in the playlist. Or tap Shuffle at the top of the list to hear a song from that playlist (and all subsequent songs) at random. That's all there is to selecting and playing a song from a playlist.

Artistic license

Now let's find and play a song by the artist's name instead of by playlist. Tap the Artists icon at the bottom of the screen and an alphabetical list of artists appears.

If the list is longer than one screen, you can, of course, flick upwards to scroll down or flick downwards to scroll up. But there are easier ways to find an artist. . . .

At the top of the screen, above the All Albums title, you can see a search field. Tap it, and type the name of the artist you want to find. Now tap the Search button to see a list of all matching artists.

Another way to find an artist is to tap one of the little letters on the right side of the screen to jump directly to artists that start with that letter. In Figure 5-1, for example, that letter is *R*.

Notice that a magnifying glass appears above the *A* on the right side of the screen. Tap it to jump directly to the search field.

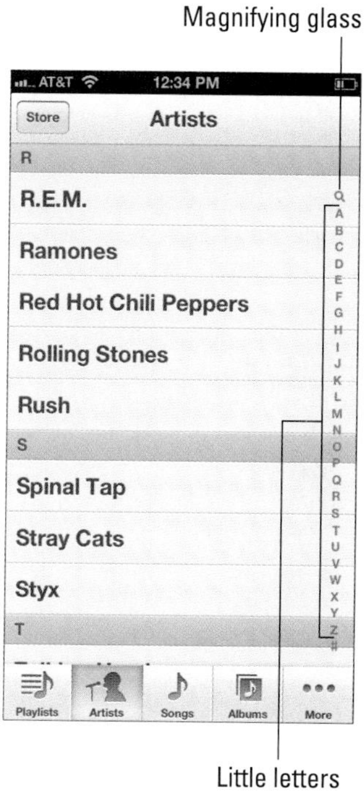

Magnifying glass

Little letters

Figure 5-1: Tap the *R* on the right side of the screen to jump to an artist's name that begins with *R*.

Tap an artist's name, and one of two things occurs:

- ✓ **If you have songs from more than one album by an artist in your music library:** A list of albums appears. Tap an album to see a list of the songs it contains. Or tap the first item in the list of albums — All Songs — to see a list of all songs on all albums by that artist.

- ✓ **If all songs in your music library by that artist are on the same album or aren't associated with a specific album:** A list of all songs by that artist appears.

Either way, just tap a song and it begins to play.

Song selection

Next, let's find a song by its title and play it. Tap the Songs icon at the bottom of the screen and a list of songs appears. You find songs the same ways you find artists: flick upward or downward to scroll; use the search field at the top of the list; or tap a little letter on the right side of the screen.

If you're not sure which song you want to listen to, try this: Tap the shuffle button at the top of the list between the search field and the first song title. Your iPhone now plays songs from your music library at random.

Album selection

Your iPhone also groups your music by album. Tap the Albums icon at the bottom of the screen and a list of albums is displayed, complete with cover art. Again, use the now-familiar Music controls to navigate through the list: flick upward or downward to scroll; use the search field at the top of the list; or tap a little letter on the right side of the screen.

When you've found the album that fits your mood, tap it to display the songs and then tap the desired track to play it.

(Home) Share and share alike

One of the best features Apple introduced in 2010 (at least in our humble opinions) is Home Sharing, which lets you use your iPhone to listen to music and watch movies, TV shows, and other media content in your computer's iTunes library.

The gotcha is that Home Sharing is available only if your iPhone and your computer are on the same Wi-Fi network.

To make Home Sharing work for you, you have to enable it on your computer and on your iPhone. To set up Home Sharing on your computer, first launch iTunes and then Choose Advanced⇨Turn On Home Sharing. Type your Apple ID and password in the appropriate fields and click the Create Home Share button. As long as iTunes is open, your iTunes library remains available for Home Sharing on your Wi-Fi network.

Now, to enable it on your iPhone, tap Settings⇨Music and type the same Apple ID and password you used to enable Home Sharing in iTunes. Tap the Home button when you're finished, tap Music⇨More⇨Shared, and tap the name of your iTunes library.

Here's the cool part: When you tap one of the icons at the bottom of the screen, rather than seeing the playlists, artists, songs, albums, and such that are stored on your iPhone, you instead see the playlists, artists, songs, albums, and so on in the iTunes library on your computer.

You continue to see the shared content in the Music app as long as your iPhone remains connected to the Wi-Fi network. If you want to switch back to the music stored on your iPhone, just reverse the process you used to select your iTunes library (tap More⇨Shared, and then tap My iPhone instead of the name of your iTunes library).

Taking Control of Your Tunes

Now that you have the basics down, take a look at some other things you can do with the Music app.

Go with the (Cover) Flow

Finding tracks by playlist, artist, or song is cool, but finding them with Cover Flow is even cooler. Cover Flow lets you browse your music collection by its album artwork. To use Cover Flow, turn your iPhone sideways (long edges parallel to the ground), tap Music, and Cover Flow fills the screen, as shown in Figure 5-2.

Flipping through your cover art in Cover Flow is simple. All you have to do is drag or flick your finger left or right on the screen and the covers go flying by. Flick or drag quickly and the covers whiz by; flick or drag slowly and the covers move leisurely. Or, tap a particular cover on the left or right of the current (centered) cover and that cover jumps to the center.

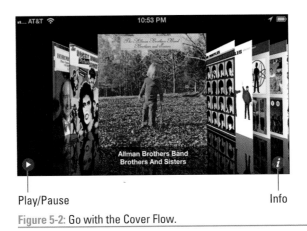

Play/Pause   Info

Figure 5-2: Go with the Cover Flow.

Try it — you'll like it! Here's how to put Cover Flow to work for you:

- ✔ **To see tracks (songs) on an album:** Tap the cover when it's centered or tap the info button (the little *i*) in the lower-right corner of the screen. The track list appears.

- ✔ **To play a track:** Tap its name in the list. If the list is long, scroll by dragging or flicking up and down on it.

- ✔ **To go back to Cover Flow:** Tap the title bar at the top of the track list or tap the little *i* button again.

- ✔ **To play or pause the current song:** Tap the Play/Pause button in the lower-left corner.

If no cover art exists for an album in your collection, the iPhone displays a plain-looking cover decorated with a single musical note. The name of the album appears below this generic cover.

And that, friends, is all there is to the iPhone's cool Cover Flow mode.

Flow's not here right now

As you saw earlier in this chapter, when you hold your iPhone vertically (the short edges are parallel to the ground) and tap the Playlists, Artists, or Songs button, you see a list rather than Cover Flow.

Along the same lines, when you're listening to music, the controls you see are different depending on which way you hold your iPhone. When you hold your iPhone vertically, as shown in Figure 5-3, you see controls that don't appear when you hold your iPhone sideways. Furthermore, the controls you see when viewing the Playlists, Artists, Albums, or Songs lists are slightly different from the controls you see when a song is playing.

Back   Switch to Track List

Playhead   Shuffle

Scrubber bar

Genius

Volume

Play/Pause

Next Track/Fast Forward

Restart/Previous Track/Rewind

Sample callout

Figure 5-3: Hold your iPhone vertically when you play a track, and you see these controls.

Here's another cool side effect of holding your iPhone vertically: If you add lyrics to a song in iTunes on your computer (by selecting the song, choosing File⟩Get Info, and then pasting or typing the lyrics into the Lyrics tab in the Info window), the lyrics are displayed along with the cover art.

Here's how to use the controls that appear when the iPhone is vertical:

- **Back button:** Tap to return to whichever list you used last — Playlists, Artists, Albums, or Songs.

- **Switch to track list button:** Tap to switch to a list of tracks.

  If you don't see the next three controls — the Repeat button, the Scrubber bar, and the Shuffle button — tap the album cover once to make them appear.

- **Repeat button:** Tap once to repeat songs in the current album or list. The button turns blue. Tap it again to play the current song repeatedly; the blue button displays the number 1 when it's in this mode. Tap the button again to turn off this feature. The button goes back to its original gray color.

- **Scrubber bar:** Drag the little dot (the playhead) along the Scrubber bar to skip to any point within the song.

- **Genius button:** Tap once and a Genius Playlist appears with 25 songs that iTunes thinks will go great with the song that's playing.

- **Shuffle button:** Tap once to shuffle songs and play them in random order. The button turns blue when shuffling is enabled. Tap it again to play songs in order again. The button goes back to its original color — gray.

- **Restart/previous track/rewind button:** Tap once to go to the beginning of the track. Tap this button twice to go to the start of the preceding track in the list. Touch and hold this button to rewind the song at double speed.

- **Play/pause button:** Tap to play or pause the song.

- **Next track/fast forward button:** Tap to skip to the next track in the list. Touch and hold this button to fast-forward through the song at double speed.

- **AirPlay selector icon:** AirPlay is a wicked cool bit of technology baked into every copy of iOS since version 4.2.

It enables you to wirelessly stream music, photos, and video to AirPlay-enabled devices such as Apple's AirPort Express Wi-Fi base station, second and third-generation Apple TVs, plus certain third-party devices that have AirPlay technology, including (but not limited to) speakers and receivers. You may or may not see the AirPlay Selector icon on your screen (it's a small rectangle with an upward-pointing arrow that sits to the right of the Next Track/Fast Forward button). The icon appears only when your iPhone detects an AirPlay-enabled device on the same Wi-Fi network.

✏ **Volume control:** Drag the little dot left or right to reduce or increase the volume level.

When you tap the switch to track list button, the iPhone screen and the controls change, as shown in Figure 5-4.

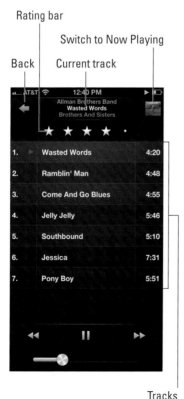

Rating bar

Switch to Now Playing

Back | Current track

Tracks

Figure 5-4: Tap the switch to track list button, and these new controls appear.

Here's how to use *those* controls:

- **Switch to Now Playing button:** Tap the tiny album cover icon at the top right of the screen to switch to the Now Playing screen for the current track.

- **Rating bar:** Drag across the rating bar to rate the current track using zero to five stars. The track shown in Figure 5-4 has a four-star rating.

The tracks are the songs in the current list (album, playlist, or artist, for example), and the current track indicator shows you which song is now playing (or paused). Tap any song in a track list to play it.

Customizing Your Audio Experience

In this section, we cover some Music features designed to make your listening experience more enjoyable.

Setting preferences

You can change a few preference settings to customize your iPhone-as-an-iPod experience.

Play all songs at the same volume level

The iTunes Sound Check option automatically adjusts the level of songs so that they play at the same volume relative to each other. That way, one song never blasts out your ears even if the recording level is much louder than that of the song before or after it. To tell the iPhone to use these volume settings, you first have to turn on the feature in iTunes on your computer. Here's how to do that:

1. **Choose iTunes⇨Preferences (Mac) or Edit⇨Preferences (PC).**

2. **Click the Playback tab.**

3. **Select the Sound Check check box to enable it.**

Now you need to tell the iPhone to use the Sound Check settings from iTunes. Here's how to do *that:*

1. **Tap the Settings icon on the iPhone's Home screen.**

2. **Tap Music in the list of settings.**

3. **Tap Sound Check to turn it on.**

Choose an equalizer setting

An *equalizer* increases or decreases the relative levels of specific frequencies to enhance the sound you hear. Some equalizer settings emphasize the bass (low end) notes in a song; other equalizer settings make the higher frequencies more apparent. The iPhone has more than a dozen equalizer presets, with names such as Acoustic, Bass Booster, Bass Reducer, Dance, Electronic, Pop, and Rock. Each one is ostensibly tailored to a specific type of music.

The way to find out whether you prefer using equalization is to listen to music while trying out different settings. To do that, first start listening to a song you like. Then, while the song is playing, follow these steps:

1. **Tap the Home button on the front of your iPhone.**

2. **Tap the Settings icon on the Home screen.**

3. **Tap Music in the list of settings.**

4. **Tap EQ in the list of Music settings.**

5. **Tap different EQ presets (Pop, Rock, R&B, or Dance, for example) and listen carefully to the way it changes how the song sounds.**

6. **When you find an equalizer preset that you think sounds good, tap the Home button and you're finished.**

If you don't like any of the presets, tap Off at the top of the EQ list to turn off the equalizer.

Set a volume limit for music (and videos)

You can instruct your iPhone to limit the loudest listening level for audio or video. To do so, here's the drill:

1. **Tap the Settings icon on the Home screen.**

2. **Tap Music in the list of settings.**

3. **Tap Volume Limit in the list of Music settings.**

4. **Drag the slider to adjust the maximum volume level to your liking.**

The Volume Limit setting limits only the volume of music. It doesn't apply to audiobooks. And, although the setting works with any headset, headphones, or speakers plugged into the headset jack on your iPhone, it doesn't affect sound played on your iPhone's internal speaker.

Enable the shake to shuffle option

Shake to Shuffle is an unusual setting that does just what its name implies — let's you shake your iPhone to listen to a different song selected at random. Here's how to enable this setting:

1. **Tap the Settings icon on the Home screen.**

2. **Tap Music in the list of settings.**

3. **Tap the Shake to Shuffle to turn it on.**

Shake to shuffle. How can you not love a feature like that?

Making a playlist

Of course you can make playlists in iTunes and sync them with your iPhone; but you can also create playlists on your iPhone when you're out and about. Here's how:

1. **Tap the Music icon in the lower-right corner of the Home screen.**

2. **Tap the Playlists button at the bottom of the screen.**

    If you've replaced Playlists with another icon as described previously, tap More and then tap Playlists.

3. **Tap the Add Playlist item in the list.**

    Music displays a New Playlist box.

4. **Type a name for your new playlist and then tap Save.**

    An alphabetical list of all songs on your iPhone appears. A little + appears to the right of each song.

5. **Tap the + sign next to a song name to add the song to your new playlist.**

   To add all these songs to your playlist, tap the Add All Songs item at the top of the list.

6. **Tap the Done button in the upper-right corner.**

If you create a playlist and then sync your iPhone with your computer, that playlist remains on your iPhone and also appears in iTunes on your computer.

Playlists remain until you delete them from iTunes or on your iPhone. To remove a playlist in iTunes, select the playlist's name in the source list and then press Delete or Backspace. To remove a playlist on your iPhone, swipe from left to right across the playlist and then tap the red Delete button.

You can also edit playlists on your iPhone. To do so, tap the Playlists icon at the bottom of the screen (or tap More and then tap Playlists), and then tap the playlist you want to edit. Three buttons appear near the top of the screen — Edit, Clear, and Delete — with the songs in the playlist listed below them.

Tap Clear to remove all the songs from this playlist; tap Delete to delete this playlist from your iPhone. Or tap Edit to do any (or all) of the following:

- **To move a song up or down in the playlist:** A little icon with three gray bars appears to the right of each song. Drag the icon up to move the song higher in the list or drag down to move the song lower in the list.

- **To add more songs to the playlist:** Tap the plus button in the upper-left corner.

- **To delete a song from the playlist:** Tap the minus sign to the left of the song name. Note that deleting a song from the playlist doesn't remove the song from your iPhone.

When you finish editing, tap the Done button. That's all there is to creating and managing playlists on your iPhone.

Use your voice to control your iPod

If you have an iPhone 3GS, 4/4S, or 5, you can boss your music around using nothing but your voice. Hold down the Home button for a few seconds until the Voice Control screen (iPhone 3GS and 4) or Siri screen (iPhone 4S and 5) appears. Here are the things you can say:

- **To play an album, artist, or playlist:** Say "Play." Then say "album," "artist," or "playlist" and the name.

- **To Shuffle the current playlist:** Say "Shuffle."

- **To find out more about the currently playing song:** Say "What's playing," "What song is this," "Who sings this song," or "Who is this song by?"

- **To use Genius to play similar songs:** Say "Genius, play more like this," or "Play more songs like this."

And hey, because your iPod happens to be an iPhone, you won't look stupid talking to it!

Shopping with the iTunes app

Last but certainly not least, the iTunes app lets you use your iPhone to download, buy, or rent just about anything you can download, buy, or rent with the iTunes application on your Mac or PC, including music, audiobooks, iTunes U classes, podcasts, and videos. And, if you're fortunate enough to have an iTunes gift card or gift certificate in hand, you can redeem it directly from your iPhone.

If you want to do any of those tasks, however, you must first sign in with your Apple ID:

1. **On the Home screen, tap the Settings icon.**

2. **Tap iTunes & App Store in the list of settings.**

3. **Tap Sign In.**

4. **Type your username and password and then tap OK.**

Or, in the unlikely event that you don't have an Apple ID already, do the following:

1. **On the Home screen, tap the Settings icon.**
2. **Tap iTunes & App Store in the list of settings.**
3. **Tap Create New Account.**
4. **Follow the on-screen instructions.**

After the iTunes Store knows who you are (and, more importantly, knows your credit card number, gift card balance, or PayPal info), tap the iTunes icon on your Home screen and shop until you drop.

Finding Stuff to Watch

The iPhone 5 isn't going to replace a wall-sized high-definition television as the centerpiece of your home theater. But with its glorious widescreen 4-inch display, watching movies and other videos on the iPhone can be a cinematic delight.

The video you'll watch on the iPhone generally falls into one of three categories:

> ✓ **Movies, TV shows, and music videos that you've downloaded directly to your iPhone or that reside in iTunes software on your PC or Mac that you synchronize with your iPhone.** You can watch these by tapping the Videos icon on the Home screen.
>
> The iTunes Store features dedicated sections for purchasing episodes of TV shows and movies. Typical price as of this writing is $2.99 per episode for TV shows and $9.99 to $14.99 for feature films.
>
> You can also rent some movies, typically for $2.99 or $3.99. You have 30 days to begin watching a rented flick, and 24 hours to finish once you've started. Such films appear in their own Rented Movies section on the Video app video list. The number of days before your rental expires is displayed.

✔ **The boatload of video podcasts, just about all of them free, featured in the iTunes Store.** Podcasts started out as another form of Internet radio; but instead of listening to live streams, you downloaded files onto your computer or iPod to take in at your leisure. There are still lots of audio podcasts around, but the focus here is on video. You watch podcasts using the free Podcasts app (new in iOS 6), which you need to download from the App Store. You can also take a seminar at Harvard, Stanford, and other prestigious institutions with the iTunes U app. iTunes U boasts more than 250,000 free lectures from around the world, many of them videos. Again, download the iTunes U app from the App Store — no charge!

✔ **Movies you've created in iMovie software or other software on the Mac or other programs on the PC.** Plus all other videos you have downloaded from the Internet.

You may have to prepare these videos so that they'll play on your iPhone. To do so, highlight the video in question after it resides in your iTunes library. Go to the Advanced menu in iTunes, and click Create iPod or iPhone Version.

Playing Video

Now that you know what you want to watch, here's how to watch it:

1. **On the Home screen, tap the Videos icon.**

   Your list of videos pops up. Videos are segregated by category — Movies, TV Shows, and Music Videos, although other categories such as Rented Movies may also appear. Listings are accompanied by thumbnail images and the length of the video.

2. **Flick your finger to scroll through the list, and then tap the video you want to play.**

   You may see a spinning circle for just a moment and then the video will begin.

3. **Turn the device to its side because the iPhone plays video only in landscape, or widescreen, mode.**

   For movies, this is a great thing. You can watch flicks as the filmmaker intended, in a cinematic *aspect ratio.*

4. **Now that the video is playing, tap the screen to display the controls shown in Figure 5-5.**

Playhead   Scrubber bar   Scale

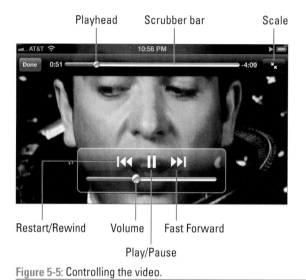

Restart/Rewind   Volume   Fast Forward

Play/Pause

Figure 5-5: Controlling the video.

5. **Tap these controls as needed:**

   • To play or pause the video, tap the Play/Pause button.

   • Drag the volume slider to the right to raise the volume and to the left to lower it. Alternatively, use the physical Volume buttons to control the audio levels. If the video is oriented properly, the buttons are to the bottom left of the iPhone.

   • Tap the Restart/Rewind button to restart the video or tap and hold the same button to rewind.

   • Tap and hold the Fast Forward button to advance the video. You can skip ahead also by dragging the playhead along the Scrubber bar.

   • Tap the Scale button to toggle between filling the entire screen with video or fitting the video to the screen. Alternatively, you can double-tap the video to go back and forth between fitting and filling the screen.

6. **Tap the screen again to make the controls go away (or just wait for them to go away on their own).**

   7. Tap Done when you've finished watching (you'll have to summon the controls back if they're not already present).

   You return to the iPhone's video menu screen.

To delete a video manually, swipe left or right over the video listing. Then tap the small red Delete button that materializes. To confirm your intention, tap the larger Delete button that appears.

6

You Oughta Be in Pictures

*T*he iPhone is a spectacular photo viewer, and the picture keeps getting better and better. The iPhone 5 has not one camera, but two: an 8-megapixel autofocus camera on the rear and a VGA camera on the front. You use the latter for FaceTime video (see Chapter 3) and for taking, dare we say, rather snappy self-portraits. The iPhone 4 was the first iPhone to add an LED flash. The 8-megapixel iPhone 4S brought even higher-resolution images, and the iPhone 5 includes an 8-megapixel camera as well. iOS 6 also introduces panorama mode, where you can shoot incredible panoramic shots with a minimum of fuss.

You can launch the camera right from the Lock screen. Drag the camera icon up to the top of the Lock screen to reveal the Camera app.

With the iPhone 3GS, 4/4S, or 5, you can also shoot your own blockbuster video! Over the next few pages, you discover how best to exploit the iPhone's camera.

Taking Your Best Shot

Like many applications on the iPhone, you find the Camera application icon on the Home screen. Unless you've moved things around, it's positioned on the upper row of icons all the way to the right and adjacent to its next-of-kin, the Photos icon. We tap both icons throughout this chapter. Go ahead and snap an image now:

1. **Tap the Camera icon on the Home screen.**

2. **Keep your eyes fixed on the iPhone's display.**

   On the screen you notice something resembling a closed camera shutter. But that shutter opens in about a second, revealing a window into what the camera lens sees.

3. **Aim the camera, using the iPhone 5's 4-inch display as your viewfinder.**

4. **When you like what you see in the frame, tap the camera icon at the bottom of the screen (see Figure 6-1) to snap the picture.**

Camera icon

Tap for preview of
last picture taken

Switch from still camera
to video camera
(3GS, 4/4s, and 5 only)

Figure 6-1: Say "Cheese."

You'll experience momentary shutter lag, so be sure to remain still. When the shutter reopens, you see the image you have just shot for just a second. Then the screen again functions as a viewfinder so that you can capture your next image.

5. **Repeat Steps 3 and 4 to capture more images.**

If you position the iPhone sideways while snapping an image, the picture is saved in landscape mode.

The iPhone Camera app button is super-sensitive. Be careful; a gentle tap is all that's required. If you have trouble keeping the camera steady, try this trick. Instead of tapping the Camera icon at the bottom of the screen, keep your finger pressed against the icon and only *release* it when you're ready to snap an image.

With the iPhone 3GS, 4/4S, or 5, you can take advantage of a feature dubbed *Tap to Focus*. Normally, the camera on these models focuses on a subject in the center of the display, which you're reminded of when you momentarily see a square in the middle of the screen. But if you tap elsewhere in the frame, perhaps on the face of your kid in the background, the iPhone shifts its focus there, adjusting the exposure and what photographers refer to as the *white balance*. For another moment or so, you see a new, smaller square over the child's face.

From the front to the rear — and back

We figure that most of the time, you'll use the main rear camera while shooting pictures (or video) because it takes higher-quality photos. But you may want to capture a shot of your own pretty face to post, say, on a social networking site such as Facebook. Not a problem. Just tap the front/rear camera button at the upper-right corner of the screen (labeled in Figure 6-2) to toggle between the front and rear cameras on the iPhone 4/4S or 5. The button doesn't appear on older iPhones, which have just a single camera.

Firing up the flash

The iPhone 4/4S and 5 are the only models with an LED (light-emitting diode) flash — or any kind of flash — so they're the only iPhones with a flash button (refer to Figure 6-2). Because no flash is associated with the front-facing camera, you won't see the button when you're using that camera. When the button is available, tap it to change the setting to On, Off, or Auto. We suggest using the Auto setting, which lets the iPhone decide when it's a good idea to fire up the flash.

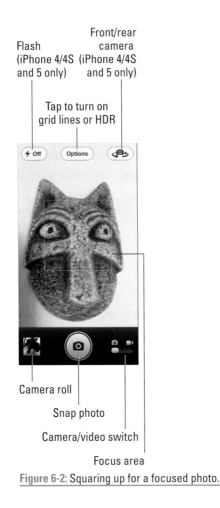

Figure 6-2: Squaring up for a focused photo.

Shooting a panorama

If you're running iOS 6, the iPhone 4S and 5 can take *panoramic* photos that encompass several screens — up to 240 degrees! (Think of the entire scope of the Grand Canyon in one photo.)

To take a panoramic photo, tap the Options button that appears at the top of the Camera app and tap the Panorama button. Follow the on-screen instructions and move your iPhone slowly and continuously from left to right across the breadth of your subject. Using your iPhone's built-in sensors, the Camera app provides a visual aid to help you maintain a steady image — keep the arrow centered on the line that appears. To finish the shot, either move through the entire 240 degrees or tap the Camera button.

Using the digital zoom

Beginning with iOS 4, you tap the screen to summon the zoom slider, and drag the slider to the right to get closer to a subject or to the left to zoom back out. In iOS 5 (and later), you can still do that, but Apple also added pinch to zoom. So now when you spread your fingers or bring them back closer together, the zoom slider appears. Continuing to pinch or unpinch has the same effect of dragging the slider to the right or left.

Importing Pictures

You don't have to use only the iPhone's digital camera to get pictures onto the device, of course. You can also synchronize photos from a PC or Macintosh using the Photos tab in the iTunes iPhone page, which is described in Chapter 2. (We assume that you already know how to get pictures onto your computer.)

When the iPhone is connected to your computer, click the iPhone in the iTunes source list and then click the Photos tab. Click the appropriate check boxes to specify the pictures and photos you want to synchronize. Or choose All Photos, Albums, Events, and Faces if you have enough storage on the iPhone.

Syncing pictures and video is a two-way process, so photos and video captured with the iPhone's digital camera can also end up in the photo library on your computer.

Where Did My Pictures Go?

So where exactly do your pictures hang out on the iPhone? The ones you snapped on iPhone end up in a photo album dubbed the *Camera Roll,* as well as two other destinations we discuss later in this chapter, *Photo Stream* and *Shared Photo Stream.* The photos you import are readily available, too, and grouped in the same albums they were on the computer.

You can get to your pictures from the Photos app or the Camera app. In the Camera app, you can see only the pictures and videos stored on the Camera Roll; in the Photos app, you can view all the pictures and videos you've imported, as well.

Let's start with the procedures for the Photos app:

1. **Tap the Photos icon on the Home screen, and then tap the Camera Roll album or any other album that appears in the list of photo albums.**

   A thumbnail displays all the photos and, if you have the iPhone 3GS, 4/4S, or 5 model, videos in the selected album, such as the one shown in Figure 6-3. (The process of shooting videos is described a little later in this chapter.)

2. **Browse through the thumbnail images in the album until you find the picture or video you want to display.**

Share, copy, or add
photo to new album

Return to Albums list

View albums

View photos
and videos by location

Figure 6-3: Your pictures at a glance.

You know when a thumbnail represents a video rather than a still image because the thumbnail displays a tiny movie camera icon and the video length. If the thumbnail you have in mind doesn't appear on this screen, flick your finger up or down to scroll through the pictures rapidly or use a slower dragging motion to pore through the images more deliberately. Buttons at the bottom of the screen enable you to view photos and videos by albums, Photo Stream, or places, as described later in this chapter.

3. **Tap the appropriate thumbnail.**

   The picture or video you selected fills the entire screen.

4. **Tap the screen again.**

   The picture controls appear, as shown in Figure 6-4. We discuss later what they do.

5. **To make the controls disappear, tap the screen again. Or just wait a few seconds, and they go away on their own.**

Slideshow

Trash image

Use image as wallpaper, e-mail it, send it via message, assign it to a contact, tweet it, or print it

Figure 6-4: Picture controls differ slightly depending on how you got there.

If you instead want to start from the Camera app, do the following:

1. Tap the Camera icon on the Home screen and then tap the Camera Roll button at the bottom-left corner of the display.

Note that the Camera Roll button displays a thumbnail of your last shot taken in the Camera Roll (refer to Figure 6-2).

The shutter closes for just an instant and the last shot you took slides up onto the screen. You see the camera controls displayed in Figure 6-4.

Note that these controls differ slightly depending on whether you got to the picture through the Camera app or the Photos app. If you started in the Camera app, you see a blue camera icon at the bottom-left corner of the screen. Tapping that icon readies you for the next shot.

If you started in Photos instead, the leftmost icon is the action icon for using the photo as wallpaper, e-mailing the photo, sending it via Message, assigning it to a contact, adding it to your Photo Stream, tweeting it, posting it to Facebook, or printing it.

If you don't see any camera controls (they disappear after a few seconds), tap the screen again. You can drag your finger from left to right to bring up earlier shots stored in the Camera Roll.

2. To transform the iPhone back into a picture taker rather than a picture viewer, make sure that the picture controls are displayed and then tap the blue Camera icon at the lower left.

Again, this option is available only if you arrived at the Camera Roll from the Camera app. If you started in the Photos app instead, you have to back out of the app altogether by pressing the Home button. Then tap the Camera app icon on the Home screen to call the iPhone's digital camera back into duty.

Swimming in the Photo Stream

As part of the iCloud service, any photos you take with the iPhone, or other iOS 5 (or later) devices such as the iPad 2, are automatically pushed to all your other devices, specifically, your PC, Mac, iPad, iPod touch, Apple TV, or another iPhone. The transfer takes place through the magic of *Photo Stream,* the antidote to the endless of problem of "I've snapped a picture, now what?"

You need not fret about storage space using Photo Stream either. The last 1,000 pictures you've taken over 30 days are held in a special *My Photo Stream* album for 30 days — enough time, Apple figures, for all your devices to connect and grab those images, because a Wi-Fi connection is your only requirement. All the pictures you've taken remain on your PC or Mac, because those machines have more capacious storage. You can always manually move images from the Photo Stream album into other albums on your iPhone or other iOS 5 or iOS 6 devices and computers.

Photos taken on the iPhone aren't whisked away into the Photo Stream until you leave the Camera app. In that way, you get a chance to delete pictures that you'd rather not have turn up everywhere.

iOS 6 introduces *Shared Photo Streams*, which require

- ✓ **iOS 6 Device:** This includes an iPhone, iPad or iPod touch running iOS 6.

- ✓ **Mac:** A Mac running OS X Mountain Lion 10.8 (with iPhoto 9.4 or later, or Aperture 3.4 or later).

- ✓ **PC:** A PC running Windows Vista or Windows 7 with the iCloud Control Panel 2.0 app or later installed.

To set up a Shared Photo Stream on your iPhone, do the following:

1. **Tap Photos and then tap the Photo Stream icon at the bottom of the screen.**

    This displays the My Photo Stream thumbnails.

2. **Tap Edit at the top-right corner of the screen.**

3. **Tap the photos you want to add to this stream.**

   Each selected photo sports a check mark.

4. **Tap the Share button and then tap the Photo Stream icon.**

   If you already have existing Shared Photo Streams, tap the New Photo Stream entry in the list.

5. **Type the email addresses for each member of the new stream.**

   To specify addresses from your Contacts list, tap the Add button next to the To field to specify the contacts. The blue Add button bears a plus sign, as shown in Figure 6-5.

6. **Tap the Name text entry box and type a name for the new stream.**

7. **To allow others that don't have iCloud.com accounts to view your stream on the web, tap the Public Website switch to turn it on.**

8. **Tap Next.**

9. **If you'd like to add a comment to be displayed with the stream, type the comment.**

10. **Tap Post to start the ball rolling.**

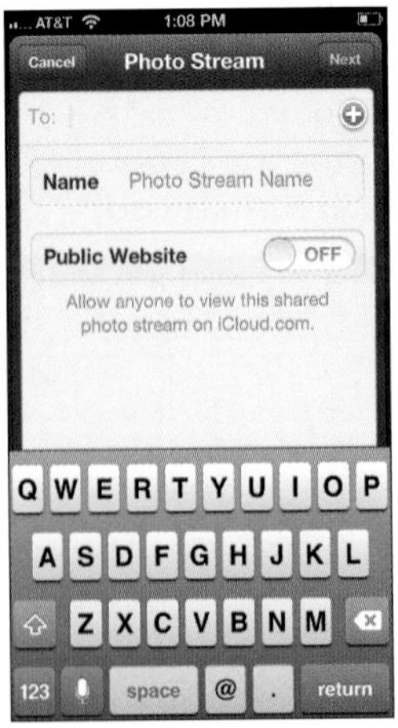

Figure 6-5: Creating a new Shared Photo Stream.

If for some reason the pictures you snap on the iPhone are not being uploaded, go to Settings, scroll down and tap Photos & Camera, and make sure both the My Photo Stream and Shared Photo Streams switches are turned on.

Admiring Pictures

Photographs are meant to be seen, of course, not buried in the digital equivalent of a shoebox. And the iPhone affords you some neat ways to manipulate, view, and share your best photos.

You already know (from the preceding section) how to find a photo and view it full-screen and bring up picture controls. But you can do a lot of maneuvering of your pictures without summoning those controls. Here are some options:

- **Skipping ahead or viewing the previous picture:** Flick your finger left or right, or tap the left or right arrow control.

- **Landscape or portrait:** The iPhone's wizardry (or more specifically, the device's accelerometer sensor) is at work. When you turn the iPhone sideways, the picture automatically reorients itself from portrait to landscape mode. Pictures shot in landscape mode fill the screen when you rotate the iPhone. Rotate the device back to portrait mode, and the picture readjusts accordingly.

- **Zoom:** Double-tap to zoom in on an image and make it larger. Do so again to zoom out and make it smaller. Alternatively, take your thumb and index finger and pinch to zoom in, or unpinch to zoom out.

- **Pan and scroll:** After you zoom in on a picture, drag it around the screen with your finger to bring the part of the image you most care about front and center.

Launching Slideshows

If you store a lot of photographs on your computer, you may be familiar with running slideshows of those images. It's a breeze to replicate the slideshow experience on the iPhone:

1. **Choose your camera roll or another album from the Photo Albums list.**

   To do so, tap the Photos icon from the Home screen or tap the Camera Roll button in the Camera application.

2. **Do one of the following:**

   - **In the Photos app,** select a picture and then tap the play icon at the bottom of the picture.

   - **In the Camera app,** tap the image in the lower-left corner of the screen to display the most recent image in the Camera Roll and then tap the play icon at the bottom of the image. If you want to start the slideshow with a different image rather than the picture that is now visible, tap the Camera Roll button at the upper-left corner of the screen. You now see a thumbnails screen, where you can tap the new starting image. Tap the play icon.

   You are taken to the Slideshow Options screen.

3. **Choose the transition effects and music (if any) that you'd like to accompany the slideshow:**

   - **Transitions:** This is what you see when you move from one photo to the next. You can choose cube, dissolve, ripple, wipe across, or wipe down.

   - **Play Music:** If you enable this option, you see the Music item appear. Tap the Music item, and you can select a song from your iPhone's Music library.

4. **Tap Start Slideshow.**

   Unless you set the slideshow to repeat, it ends automatically. Tap the screen to end it prematurely.

Special slideshow effects

You can alter the length of time each slide is shown, change the transition effects between pictures, and display images in random order.

From the Home screen, tap Settings and then scroll down and tap Photos & Camera. Then tap any of the following to make changes:

- **Play Each Slide For:** You have five choices (2 seconds, 3 seconds, 5 seconds, 10 seconds, 20 seconds). When you're finished, tap the Photos & Camera button to return to the main Settings screen for Photos.

- **Repeat:** If this option is turned on, the slideshow continues to loop until you stop it. If it's turned off, the slideshow for your Camera Roll or album plays just once. The Repeat control may be counterintuitive. If Off is showing, tap it to turn on the Repeat function. If On is showing, tap it to turn off the Repeat function.

- **Shuffle:** Turning on this feature plays photos in random order. As with the Repeat feature, tap Off to turn on shuffle or tap On to turn off random playback.

Press the Home button to leave the settings and return to the Home screen.

Touching up photos

The iPhone is never going to serve as a substitute for a high-end photo-editing program such as Adobe Photoshop. But you can do some relatively simple touch-ups, right from inside the Photos app.

Choose an image and tap Edit. At the bottom of the screen are four icons, shown in Figure 6-6 and described next:

- **Rotate:** Rotate the image counterclockwise.

- **Auto-enhance:** Let the iPhone take a stab at making your image look better. Apple lightens or darkens the picture, tweaks color saturation, and more. Tap Save if you like the result.

- **Remove red-eye:** Get rid of that annoying red-eye. Tap each eye; tap again to undo.

- **Crop:** Crop the image. By tapping the Constrain button, you can choose to crop the image through many different aspect ratio options.

Rotate | Crop

Auto-enhance

Remove red-eye

Figure 6-6: Who says you can't improve the quality of the picture?

Deleting Pictures

Some pictures are meant to be seen. Others, well . . . you can't get rid of them fast enough. Fortunately, the iPhone makes it a cinch to bury the evidence:

1. **From the Camera Roll, tap the objectionable photograph.**

2. **Tap to display the picture controls, provided they're not already displayed.**

3. **Tap the trash can icon.**

4. **Tap Delete Photo (or Cancel if you change your mind).**

The photo gets sucked into the trash can.

More (Not So) Stupid Picture Tricks

You can take advantage of the photos on the iPhone in a few more ways. In each case, you tap the picture and make sure the picture controls are displayed. Then tap the icon that looks like an arrow trying to escape from a rectangle (at the lower left side of the screen). That displays the nine choices shown in Figure 6-7.

Here's what each choice does:

✔ **Mail:** Tap Mail to automatically embed the photo in the body of an outgoing e-mail message. Use the virtual keyboard to enter the e-mail addresses, Subject line, and any comments you want to add. Tap Send to whisk away the picture and accompanying message.

✔ **Copy:** Tap the Copy button to send the photo to your iPhone clipboard. You can now paste the image into documents and other apps.

Figure 6-7: Look at what else I can do!

✔ **Message:** Apple and your provider support picture messaging through what's called MMS (Multimedia Messaging Service). Tap the Message option, and the picture is embedded in your outgoing message; you merely need to enter the phone number or name of the person to whom you're sending the picture. If that person is also using an iOS 5 (or later) device, or is using a Mac that's running OS X Lion or Mountain Lion, the photo is sent as an iMessage, which doesn't count against your texting allotment.

✔ **Assign to Contact:** If you assign a picture to someone in your Contacts list, the picture you assign pops up whenever you receive a call from that person. Tap Assign to Contact. Your list of contacts appears on the screen. Scroll through the list to find the person who matches the picture of the moment. As with the Use as Wallpaper option (described next), you can drag and resize the picture to get it just right. Then tap Set Photo.

You can also assign a photo to a contact by starting out in Contacts. Tap Phone and then tap Contacts. From Contacts, choose the person, tap Edit, and then tap Add Photo. At that point, you can take a new picture with the iPhone's digital camera or select an existing portrait from one of your onboard picture albums.

To change the picture you assigned to a person, tap his or her name in the Contacts list, tap Edit, and then tap the person's thumbnail picture, which also carries the label Edit. From there, you can take another photo with the iPhone's digital camera, select another photo from one of your albums, edit the photo you're already using (by resizing and dragging it to a new position), or delete the photo you no longer want.

✔ **Photo Stream:** Tap this icon to add the photo to a Shared Photo Stream, as described earlier in this chapter. You're prompted to choose the desired Shared Photo Stream.

Note that you do not have to tap this button to assign the photo to My Photo Stream — that's done automatically by your iPhone (as long as you're running iOS 5 or later). The Photo Stream button applies only to Shared Photo Streams that you've created manually.

✔ **Use as Wallpaper:** When you tap the Use as Wallpaper button, you see what the present image looks like as the iPhone's background picture. And, as Figure 6-8 shows, you're given the opportunity to move the picture around and resize it, through the now familiar action of dragging or pinching against the screen with your fingers. When you're satisfied with what the wallpaper looks like, tap the Set button. Options appear that enable you to use the photo as wallpaper for the Lock screen, the Home screen, or both. Per usual, you also have the option to tap Cancel.

Figure 6-8: Beautifying the iPhone with wallpaper.

✓ **Twitter:** Lots of people send pictures via Twitter these days. The iPhone makes it breeze. Tap Tweet and your picture is embedded in an outgoing tweet. Just add your words, sticking to Twitter's character limit of 140. Don't forget to configure at least one Twitter account in the Twitter pane within Settings — you should also install the Twitter app.

✓ **Facebook:** Tap this icon to embed the image in a Facebook posting, complete with any comment you might like to add. Again, you need to configure your Facebook account in the Facebook pane within Settings, and you need to install the Facebook app on your iPhone.

✓ **Print:** If you have a wireless AirPrint-capable printer, tap Print to print the photo. You can choose how many copies of the print you wish to duplicate.

Shooting Video

The iPhone 4S and 5 both produce high-definition video at what techies refer to as *1080p.* (The iPhone 4 played in the high-def league, too, but at the lower *720p* video resolution standard.) Moreover, the 4S and 5 help compensate for any shakes via video image stabilization. And through a process known as *temporal noise reduction,* you can shoot terrific video even in dim light.

Here's how to shoot video on the 3GS, 4/4S, or 5 phone models. Note that you can capture video in portrait or landscape mode:

1. **Tap the Camera icon on the Home screen.**

2. **Drag the little on-screen button at the bottom-right corner of the display from the camera position to the video camera position, as shown in Figure 6-9.**

3. **Tap the red record button at the bottom center to begin shooting a scene.**

   The button blinks, and you see a counter timing the length of your video.

4. **When you're finished, tap the red button again to stop recording.**

   Your video is automatically saved to your Camera Roll, alongside any other saved videos and still pictures.

Front/rear camera
(iPhone 4/4S and 5 only)

Flash (iPhone
4/4S and 5 only)

Camera Roll

Start or stop
capturing video

Camera/video
switch

Figure 6-9: Who better to capture on video?

You can tap the LED flash button to shine a light while you record video. And, as with taking digital stills, you can switch from the front to the rear camera before starting to shoot video. But you can't switch from the front to back camera while you are capturing video.

Editing what you shot

Likely, you captured some really great photos and some stuff that belongs on the cutting room floor. That's not a problem because you can perform simple edits right on your iPhone 3GS, iPhone 4/4S, and iPhone 5:

1. **Tap a video recording to bring up the on-screen controls shown in Figure 6-10.**

2. **Drag the start and end points along the timeline to select only the video you want to keep. Hold your finger over the section to expand the timeline to make it easier to apply your edits.**

   You can tap the Play button to preview the edit.

Drag either edge to trim

Tap to trim clip or create
newly trimmed video

Figure 6-10: Trimming video.

3. Tap Trim to save your changes.

You have the option to trim the original clip or to save the trimmed result as a new clip.

If you choose Trim Original, make sure you're satisfied with your edit. You can't undo this action.

Sharing video

Unlike other video on your iPhone, you can play back what you've just shot in portrait or landscape mode. And if the video is any good (and why wouldn't it be), you're likely going to want to share it with others. To do so, bring up the playback controls by tapping the screen; then tap the Action icon (it's the second icon at the bottom of the screen, shown in the left margin here). You can e-mail the video, enclose it in an MMS or iMessage, or send it to YouTube.

7

Surfing, Setting Reminders, Working with Passbook and Using E-Mail

In This Chapter

▶ Surfing the 'Net

▶ Opening and displaying web pages

▶ Using Reminders to jog your memory

▶ Setting up and using Passbook

▶ Setting up your e-mail accounts

▶ Sending e-mail messages

▶ Reading and managing e-mail messages

*F*or years, the cell phone industry has been offering a watered-down mobile version of the Internet, but the approaches have fallen far short of what you've come to experience on your computer. With the iPhone, however, Apple has managed to replicate the real-deal Internet. Web pages look like web pages on a Windows PC or Macintosh, right down to swanky graphics and pictures. In this chapter, you find out how to navigate through cyberspace on your iPhone.

Surfin' Safari

A version of Apple Safari web browser is a major reason the Net is the 'Net on the iPhone. Safari for the Mac and, more recently, for Windows, is one of the best web browsers in the computer business. In our view, it has no rival as a cell phone browser.

Exploring the browser

It is worth starting our cyber-expedition with a quick tour of the Safari browser. Take a gander at Figure 7-1.

Blasting into cyberspace

When you tap the address field, the virtual keyboard appears. You may notice one thing about the keyboard right off the bat. Because so many web addresses end with the suffix *.com*, the virtual keyboard has a dedicated .com key. For other common web suffixes — *.edu, .net, .ee,* and *.org* — press and hold the .com key and choose the relevant suffix.

Of equal importance, both the . (period) and the / (slash) are on the virtual keyboard because you frequently use them when you enter web addresses. Note, however, that there's no space bar — spaces aren't allowed in a web address.

The moment you tap a single letter, you see a list of web addresses that match those letters. For example, if you tap the letter *E*, you see web listings for EarthLink, eBay, and so on.

When you tap a letter, the iPhone suggests web sites either from the web sites you've already bookmarked (and synced) from Safari or Internet Explorer on your computer or from your History list — those cyber-destinations you've recently hung your hat in.

Search Google,
Yahoo!, or Bing

Address field

Reload web page

Pages

View Bookmarks
or Reading List

Bookmark/Reading
List/Home Screen/Mail/
Tweet/Facebook/Print

Next web page

Previous web page

Figure 7-1: The iPhone's Safari browser.

Go ahead and open your first web page now:

1. **Tap the Safari icon at the bottom of the Home screen.**

2. **Tap the address field (shown in Figure 7-1).**

   If you can't see the address field, tap the status bar or scroll to the top of the screen.

3. **Begin typing the web address (URL) on the virtual keyboard that slides up from the bottom of the screen.**

4. **Do one of the following:**

   a. *To accept one of the bookmarked (or other) sites that shows up on the list, merely tap the name.*

   Safari automatically fills in the URL in the address field and takes you where you want to go.

   b. *Keep tapping the proper keyboard characters until you've entered the complete web address for the site you have in mind, and then tap Go at the bottom-right corner of the keyboard.*

   It's not necessary to type *www* at the beginning of a URL. So if you want to visit www.theonion.com (for example), typing **theonion.com** is sufficient.

Even though Safari on the iPhone can render web pages the way they're meant to be displayed on a computer, you may run into a site that serve ups the light, or mobile, version of the web site. Graphics may be stripped down on such sites. (For example, CNN.com detects the mobile version of Safari when you visit and presents a simplified site.)

Seeing pages more clearly

Now that you know how to open up a web page, we'll show you how radically simple it is to zoom in on the pages so you can read what you want to read and see what you want to see, without enlisting a magnifying glass.

Try these neat tricks:

- **Double-tap the screen so that that portion of the text fills up the entire screen:** It'll take just a second before the screen comes into focus. Check out Figure 7-2. It shows two views of the same *Sports Illustrated* web page. In the first view, you see what the page looks like when you first arrive. In the second, you see how the middle column takes over the screen after you double-tapped on it. To return to the first view, double-tap the screen again.

- **Pinch the page:** Sliding your thumb and index finger together and then spreading them apart also zooms in and out of a page. Again, wait just a moment for the screen to come into focus.

- **Press down on a page and drag it in all directions, or flick through a page from top to bottom.**

- **Rotate the iPhone to its side:** Watch what happens to the White House web site shown in Figure 7-3. It reorients from portrait to a widescreen view. The keyboard is also wider, making it a little easier to enter a new URL.

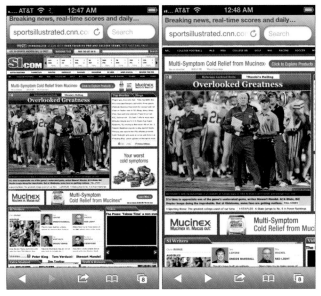

Figure 7-2: A double-tap zooms in and out.

Figure 7-3: Going wide.

Using the Reading List

iOS 5 introduced the Safari *Reading List*, which enables you to save interesting pages you encounter during a surfing session for later reading. Tap the Action icon at the bottom of the Safari screen — it's the square with the arrow jumping out of it in the middle of the row that's labeled as *Add Bookmarks/ Reading list. . ..* in Figure 7-1 — and tap Add to Reading List. You can do this as often as you like while surfing.

To display the Reading List, tap the Bookmarks icon at the bottom of the screen (it looks like an open book) and choose Reading List. Tap a story to view the page, and the story is automatically removed from the list.

Putting Reminders to Work

It's time to banish that old appointment book (or even worse, that stack of tiny scraps of paper in your wallet or purse). With the Reminders app that arrived with iOS5, your iPhone can hold your to-do list and keep it updated automatically across all your iOS devices, via iCloud. The Reminders app works with OS X Calendar and Outlook too, keeping track of events between your computer and your iPhone.

To get started, tap the Reminders icon on the Home screen, and you see the List view shown in Figure 7-4. To add a new reminder for a specific day, tap the day on the calendar strip at the bottom of the screen to highlight it, and then tap the Add icon (the plus sign) in the top-right corner of the screen. The virtual keyboard appears, enabling you to type the text of your reminder. When you're finished, tap the Done button in the upper-right corner. Now you can tap the item itself, which displays the Details dialog. From here, you can set an audible reminder (with a corresponding notification), choose to be reminded when you enter or leave a location, and specify whether this is a repeating event.

After you take care of a to-do item, tap the check box next to it to indicate that it's been completed. To delete a reminder, display the Details dialog again and tap Delete.

You can always jump back to today's reminder page by tapping Today.

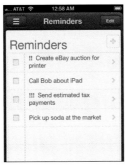

Figure 7-4: The Reminders screen.

To search for a specific reminder, tap the Calendar icon to switch to Calendar view; tap within the Search Reminders box and type the text you want to match.

Using Your Passbook

The arrival of iOS 6 brought Passbook to the iPhone. You can think of this new feature as an "electronic wallet" for storing airline boarding passes, event tickets, gift and loyalty cards, and coupons.

The idea is simple: You buy a ticket for an airline flight, a movie, or a rock concert (or earn a coupon or gift card) from a participating retailer, which is then stored within Passbook as a *pass*. When you need to redeem a pass — for example, when you enter a concert venue — you select that pass and Passbook displays a QR or bar code that can be scanned at the gate.

Passbook requires iCloud, which means you need — you guessed it — an Apple ID.

In fact, Passbook can even use your location to display the code automatically when you need it, even if your iPhone is locked. (You arrive at the movie theater, and because you have a ticket you've bought online through Fandango, Passbook automatically displays the QR code. *Sweet!*)

First, however, you must add the apps to your iPhone for each Passbook retailer that you frequent. Tap the Passbook icon on the Home screen and then tap the App Store button at the bottom of the screen. Your iPhone immediately displays the Apps for Passbook list, where you can select from companies like Target, American Airlines, Ticketmaster, and Fandango. Tap the Free button next to each app that you want to download. — they appear as separate apps on your iPhone, just like any other app you install. (You can explore each retailer app to see what features they include.)

Now you can add passes to Passbook from within those retailer apps — in many cases, you can also add passes from a participating retailer's website.

No matter how you obtain a pass, it appears immediately when you run the Passbook app. To review details on any pass, tap it and then tap the *i* button that appears at the lower-right corner of the display.

If a location doesn't support the automatic display of a Passbook pass, you can always use the pass manually: tap the pass in the list to display the code and then allow the code to be scanned.

Setting Up E-Mail

One of the niftiest things your iPhone can do is send and receive real, honest-to-gosh e-mail, using Mail, its modern e-mail application. It's designed not only to send and receive text e-mail messages, but also to handle rich HTML e-mail messages — formatted e-mail messages complete with font and type styles and embedded graphics.

Furthermore, your iPhone can read several types of file attachments, including PDF, Microsoft Word, PowerPoint, and Excel documents, as well as stuff produced through Apple's own iWork software. Better still, all this sending and receiving of text, graphics, and documents can happen in the background, so you can surf the web or talk to a friend while your iPhone quietly and efficiently handles your e-mail behind the scenes.

To use Mail you need an e-mail address. If you have broadband Internet access (that is, a cable modem or DSL), you probably received one or more e-mail addresses when you signed up. If you are one of the handful of readers who doesn't already have an e-mail account, you can get one for free from Yahoo! (`http://mail.yahoo.com`), Google (`http://mail.google.com`), Microsoft (`Hotmail.com`), AOL (`http://www.aol.com`), and many other service providers.

Set up your account the easy way

Chapter 2 explains the option of automatically syncing the e-mail accounts on your computer with your iPhone. If you chose that option, your e-mail accounts should be configured on your iPhone already. You may proceed directly to the "Sending E-Mail" section.

If you have not yet chosen that option but would like to set up your account the easy way now, go to Chapter 2 and read that section, sync your iPhone, and then you, too, may proceed directly to the "Sending E-Mail" section.

Set up your account the less easy way

If you don't want to sync the e-mail accounts on your computer, you can set up an e-mail account on your iPhone manually. It's not quite as easy as clicking a box and syncing your iPhone, but it's not rocket science either.

If you have no e-mail accounts on your iPhone, the first time you launch Mail you're walked through the following procedure. If you have one or more e-mail accounts on your iPhone already and want to add a new account manually, start by tapping Settings on the Home screen, and then tap Mail, Contacts, Calendars, and tap Add Account.

You should now be staring at the Add Account screen. Proceed to one of the next two sections, depending on your e-mail account.

Yahoo!, Google, Microsoft, AOL, or iCloud.

If your account is with Yahoo!, Google (Gmail), AOL, Microsoft Exchange, Microsoft Hotmail, or Apple's own iCloud service, tap the appropriate button on the Add Account screen now. If your account is with a provider other than these four, tap the Other button and skip ahead to the next section.

Enter your name, e-mail address, and password, as shown in Figure 7-5. There's a field for a description of this account (such as work or personal), but it tends to fill in automatically with the same contents in the Address field unless you tell it differently.

Optional field

Figure 7-5: Just fill 'em in, tap Save, and you're ready to rock.

Tap the Next button in the top-right corner of the screen. You're finished. Your e-mail provider will verify your credentials. If you pass muster, that's all there is to setting up your account.

Another provider

If your e-mail account is with a provider other than Yahoo!, Google, AOL, Microsoft, or iCloud, you have a bit more work ahead of you. You're going to need a bunch of information about your e-mail account that you may not know or have handy.

We suggest that you scan the following instructions, note the items you don't know, and go find the answers before you continue. To find the answers, look at the documentation you received when you signed up for your e-mail account or visit the account provider's web site and search there.

Here's how you set up an account:

1. **On the Add Account screen, tap the Other button.**

2. **Under Mail, tap Add Mail Account; fill in the Name, Address, Password, and Description in the appropriate fields, same as if you were setting up an account with one of the providers mentioned earlier.**

3. **Tap Next.**

   With any luck, that's all you have to do, although you may have to endure a spinning cursor for a while as the iPhone attempts to retrieve information and validate your account with your provider. Otherwise, continue on with Step 4.

4. **Tap the button at the top of the screen that denotes the type of e-mail server this account uses: IMAP or POP, as shown in Figure 7-6.**

5. **Fill in the Internet host name for your incoming mail server, which should look something like mail.** *providername***.com.**

6. **Fill in your username and password.**

Figure 7-6: If you don't use Yahoo!, Google, AOL, Microsoft, or iCloud, you may have a few more fields to fill in.

7. **Enter the Internet host name for your outgoing mail server, which should look something like smtp.** *providername***.com.**

    You may have to scroll down to the bottom of the screen to see the outgoing mail server fields.

8. **Enter your username and password in the provided fields.**

9. **Tap the Next button in the upper-right corner to create the account.**

 Some outgoing mail servers don't need your username and password. The fields for these items on your iPhone note that they are optional. Still, we suggest that you fill them in anyway. It will save you from having to add them later if your outgoing mail server *does* require an account name and password, which many do these days.

Now that your account or accounts are set up, let's look at how to use your iPhone to send e-mail.

Sending E-Mail

There are several subspecies of messages: pure text, text with a photo, a partially finished message you want to save and complete later (called a draft), a reply to an incoming message, forwarding an incoming message to someone else, and so on. The following sections examine these subsets one at a time.

Sending an all-text message

To compose a new e-mail message, tap Mail on your Home screen. You should see a screen that looks pretty much like the one in Figure 7-7 — if not, tap your primary mail account name in the Accounts section.

Tap to see other e-mail accounts

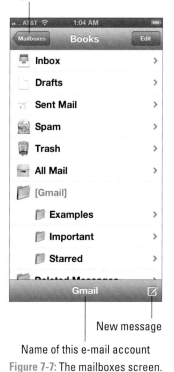

New message

Name of this e-mail account

Figure 7-7: The mailboxes screen.

Don't worry if yours doesn't look exactly like this or if your folders have different names.

Now, to create a new message, follow these steps:

1. **Tap the New Message button (labeled in Figure 7-7) in the lower-right corner of the screen.**

   A screen like the one shown in Figure 7-8 appears.

Begin typing   Select a contact

...AT&T 🗢	11:00 PM	🔋
Cancel	**New Message**	Send

To: ⊕

Cc/Bcc, From: books@mail.com

Subject:

Sent from my iPhone

Q W E R T Y U I O P
A S D F G H J K L
⇧ Z X C V B N M ⌫
123 🎤 space @ . return

Figure 7-8: The New Message screen appears ready for you to start typing the recipient's name.

2. **Type the names or e-mail addresses of the recipients in the To: field, or tap the + button to the right of To: to choose a contact or contacts from your iPhone's address book.**

3. **(Optional) Tap the field labeled Cc/Bcc/From:. Doing so breaks these out into separate Cc:, Bcc:, and From: fields.**

   The Cc/Bcc: label stands for *carbon copy/blind carbon copy.* If you haven't used Bcc: before, it enables you to include a recipient on the message that other recipients can't see has been included. Tap the respective Cc: or Bcc: field to type in names. Or tap the + that appears in those fields to add a contact.

   If you start typing an e-mail address, e-mail addresses that match what you've typed appear in a list below the To: or Cc: field. If the correct one is in the list, tap it to use it.

4. **Type a subject in the Subject field.**

   The subject is optional, but it's considered poor form to send an e-mail message without one.

5. **Type your message in the message area.**

   The message area is immediately below the Subject field.

   Don't forget that snappy Dictation key on your iPhone's virtual keyboard! If you're running iOS 5 (or later), tap the key with the microphone symbol and begin speaking. When you're through dictating the message, tap the Done button.

6. **Tap the Send button in the top-right corner of the screen.**

Your message wings its way to its recipients almost immediately. If you are not in range of a Wi-Fi or cellular data network when you tap Send, the message is sent the next time you are in range of one of these networks

Replying to or forwarding a message

When you receive a message and want to reply to it, open the message and then tap the Reply/Reply All/Forward button, which looks like a curved arrow at the bottom of the screen, as shown in Figure 7-9. Then tap the Reply, Reply All, or Forward button — you can also print the message by tapping this button.

The Reply button creates a blank e-mail message addressed to the sender of the original message. The Reply All button creates a blank e-mail message addressed to the sender and all other recipients of the original message (the button only appears with multiple recipients). In both cases the subject is retained with a *Re:* prefix added. So if the original subject was *iPhone Tips,* the reply's subject would be *Re: iPhone Tips.*

Tapping the Forward button creates an unaddressed e-mail message that contains the text of the original message. Add the e-mail address(es) of the person or people you want to forward the message to, and then tap Send. In this case, instead of a *Re:* prefix, the subject is preceded by *Fwd:.* So this time the subject would be *Fwd: iPhone Tips.*

To send your reply or forwarded message, tap the Send button as usual.

Next Message

Previous Message

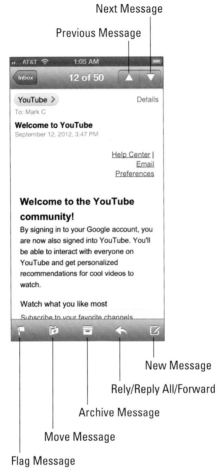

New Message

Rely/Reply All/Forward

Archive Message

Move Message

Flag Message

Figure 7-9: Reading and managing an e-mail message.

Working with Messages

The other half of the mail equation is receiving and reading the stuff. You can tell when you have unread mail by looking at the Mail icon, in the bottom of your Home screen. The cumulative number of unread messages appears in a little red circle on the top-right of the icon.

New message notifications also appear on the Notification Center — swipe down from the top of the screen to display it.

Reading messages

Tap the Mail icon to summon the Mailboxes screen. At the top of the Inboxes section is the All Inboxes inbox which, as its name suggests, is a repository for all the messages across all your accounts. (Naturally, if you have only one account within Mail, you see that account inbox instead of All Inboxes.) To read your mail, tap an inbox: either All Inboxes to examine all your messages in one unified view or an individual account to check out messages from just that account.

Now tap a message to read it. When a message is on the screen, buttons for managing incoming messages appear below it.

Managing messages

When a message is on your screen, you can do the following in addition to reading it (all buttons are labeled in Figure 7-9):

- ✒ View the next message by tapping the next message button.

- ✒ View the previous message by tapping the previous message button.

- ✒ Flag this message by tapping the Flag button, which looks like. . . well. . . a flag. You can choose to flag the message, or mark it as unread. (When you flag a message, it appears in the Inbox list with a flag icon to the left of the entry. You can use flags to mark important messages that need immediate follow-up.)

- ✒ File this message in another folder by tapping the file message button. When the list of folders appears, tap the folder where you want to file the message.

- ✒ Delete this message by tapping the delete message button. You have a chance to cancel in case you tapped the delete message button by mistake.

- ✒ Reply, reply to all, or forward this message (as discussed previously) by tapping the Reply/Reply All/Forward button.

- ✒ Create a new e-mail message by tapping the new message button.

To check for new messages in Mail under iOS 6, drag the screen down with two fingers — Mail connects with your servers and updates your message list.

You can delete e-mail messages without opening them in two ways:

- Swipe left or right across the message and then tap the red Delete button that appears to the right of the message.

- Tap the Edit button in the upper-right corner of the screen and tap the little circle to the left of each message you want to remove. Tap that Delete button to erase all the messages you'd checked off, as shown in Figure 7-10.

Tap to select a message to remove

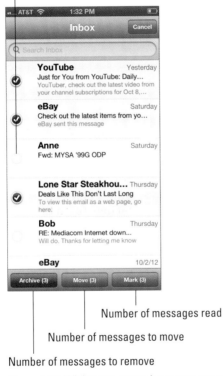

Number of messages read

Number of messages to move

Number of messages to remove

Figure 7-10: Wiping out, or moving messages, en masse.

8

Tracking with Maps, Compass, Stocks, and Weather

In This Chapter

▷ Mapping your route with Maps

▷ Course-setting with Compass

▷ Getting quotes with Stocks

▷ Watching the weather with Weather

*I*n this chapter, we look at four of the iPhone's Internet-enabled apps: Maps, Compass, Stocks, and Weather. We call them *Internet-enabled* because they display information collected over your Internet connection — whether Wi-Fi or wireless data network — in real time (or in the case of Stocks, near-real time).

Maps Are Where It's At

In the first edition of this book, we said that the Maps feature was one of the sleeper hits of our iPhone experience and an app we both use more than we expected because it's so darn handy. Since then, Maps has become better and more capable — and with the arrival of iOS 6, Apple has completely revamped this jewel of an app, improving the graphics and the functionality. With Maps, you can quickly and easily discover exactly where you are; find nearby restaurants and businesses; get spoken turn-by-turn driving, walking, and public transportation instructions from any address to any other address; take an aerial tour of a city with Flyover; and see real-time traffic information for many locations.

Finding your current location with Maps

 Let's start with something supremely simple yet extremely useful — determining your current location. At the risk of sounding like self-help gurus, here's how to find yourself: Tap the Maps icon and then tap the little arrowhead icon in the lower-left corner.

If you have an iPhone 4/4S, or 5, a pulsating blue marker indicates your location on the map when the phone's GPS is used to find your location. In addition, the Location Services indicator, a purple arrowhead, appears to the left of the battery indicator in the status bar (both are shown in Figure 8-1).

If GPS is not being used because you're out of the satellite's sight line or because you're using a first-generation iPhone (which had no GPS), a somewhat larger pale blue circle shows your approximate location. Either way, when you move around, the iPhone updates your location and adjusts the map so the location indicator stays in the middle of the screen.

If you tap or drag the map, your iPhone continues to update your location; but it won't recenter the marker, which means that the location indicator can move off the screen.

Finding a person, place, or thing

To find a person, place, or thing with Maps, tap the search field at the top of the screen to make the keyboard appear. Now type what you're looking for. You can search for addresses, zip codes, intersections, towns, landmarks, and businesses by category and by name, or combinations, such as *New York, NY 10022, pizza 60645,* or *Auditorium Shores Austin TX.*

Location Services indicator

Current location indicator

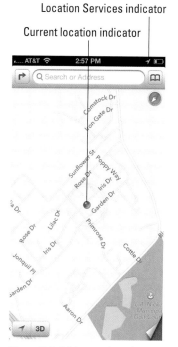

Figure 8-1: A blue marker shows your location, and an arrowhead in the status bar shows you're using GPS.

If the letters you type match names in your Contacts list, the matching contacts appear in a list below the search field. Tap a name to see a map of that contact's location. Maps is smart about it, too; it displays only the names of contacts that have a street address.

When you finish typing, tap Search. After a few seconds, a map appears. If you searched for a single location, it is marked with a single pushpin. If you searched for a category (*pizza 60645,* for example), you see multiple pushpins, one for each matching location, as shown in Figure 8-2.

Figure 8-2: Search for *pizza 60645* and you see pushpins for all nearby pizza joints.

Views, zooms, and pans

The preceding section talks about how to find just about anything with Maps. Now here's a look at some ways you can use what you find. First, find out how to work with what you see on the screen. Three views are available at any time: Standard, Satellite, and Hybrid. (Refer to Figure 8-2 for a Standard view; Figure 8-3 shows the Satellite view.) Select one view by tapping the curling page button in the lower-right corner. The map then curls back and reveals several buttons, as shown in Figure 8-4.

No matter what view you choose, you can zoom to see either more or less of the map — or scroll (pan) to see what's above, below, or to the left or right of what's on the screen:

✔ **To zoom out:** Pinch the map or *double-tap using two fingers.* To zoom out even more, pinch or double-tap using two fingers again.

Double-tapping with two fingers may be a new concept to you: Merely tap twice in rapid succession with two fingers rather than the usual one finger. That's a total of four taps, input efficiently as two taps per finger.

Figure 8-3: Satellite view of the map shown in Figure 8-2.

Figure 8-4: The map curls back to reveal these buttons.

- **To zoom in:** Unpinch the map or double-tap (the usual way — with just one finger) the spot you want to zoom in on. Unpinch or double-tap with one finger again to zoom in even more.
- **To scroll:** Flick or drag up, down, left, or right.

3D and Flyover

When you zoom in close enough in Standard view, the 3D button is enabled. You can tap it in any view to display the map from a 3D angle — no, it's not cinema-quality 3D, but it's a neat feature. To change the angle of the view, drag up or down with two fingers.

If you're viewing a map of a large city using Satellite or Hybrid view, you may see the 3D button change to the Flyover button (which looks like three skyscrapers, visible in Figure 8-3) — tap it for a real treat, as you move through the skyline with your fingertips! Figure 8-5 illustrates a favorite Flyover spot: the Empire State Building in New York City.

Figure 8-5: Welcome to the Big Apple!

As with 3D, you can drag up or down with two fingers to change the angle within Flyover.

Maps and contacts

Maps and contacts go together like peanut butter and jelly. For example, if you want to see a map of a contact's street address, tap the little bookmarks icon to the right of the search field, tap the Contacts button at the bottom of the screen, and then tap the contact's name. Or type the first few letters of the contact's name in the search field and then tap the name in the list that automatically appears below the search field.

After you find a location by typing an address into Maps, you can add that location to one of your contacts. Or you can create a new contact with a location you've found. To do either, tap the location's pushpin on the map and then tap the little > in a blue circle to the right of the location's name or description (shown for Gullivers in Figures 8-2 and 8-3) to display its Info screen (see Figure 8-6).

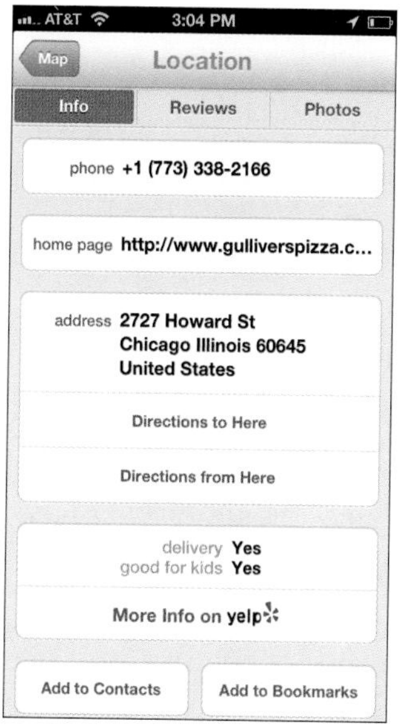

Figure 8-6: The Info screen for Gullivers Pizza.

Now tap the Add to Contacts button on the Info screen. You probably need to scroll to the bottom of the Info screen (refer to Figure 8-6, right) to see this button.

REMEMBER
You work with your contacts in two ways. One way is to tap the Contacts icon, which is in the Utilities folder on the second page of icons on the Home screen (swipe from right to left on the Home screen to see this second page). The second way is to tap the Phone icon on your Home screen and then tap the Contacts icon in the Phone screen's dock.

You can also get driving directions from most locations, including a contact's address, to most other locations, including another contact's address. You see how to do that in the "Smart map tricks" section, later in the chapter.

Timesaving map tools: Bookmarks, Recents, and Contacts

Maps offers three tools that can save you from having to type the same locations over and over. All three are in the Bookmarks screen, which appears when you tap the little bookmarks icon on the right side of the search field (refer to Figure 8-2).

At the bottom of the Bookmarks screen, you find three buttons: Bookmarks, Recents, and Contacts. The following sections give you the lowdown on these buttons.

Bookmarks

Bookmarks in the Maps app, like bookmarks in Safari, let you return to a location without typing a single character. Simply tap the little > in a blue circle to the right of the location's name or description to display the Info screen for that location. Tap the Add to Bookmarks button on the Info screen. (You may have to scroll down the Info screen to see the Add to Bookmarks button.)

You can also drop a pin anywhere on the map by tapping the curling page button in the lower-right corner, and then tapping the Drop Pin button. After you've dropped a pin, you can press and drag it anywhere on the map. When the pin is where you want it, lift your finger to drop the pin, and a banner with the location of the pin (if Maps can figure it out) and a little > in a blue circle appears. Tap the little >, and the Info screen for the dropped pin appears. Now tap the Add to Bookmarks button on the Info screen.

The info screen for a dropped pin offers the same buttons as the Info screen for a location, along with the very important Remove Pin button.

After you add a bookmark, you can recall it at any time. To do so, tap the bookmarks icon in the search field, tap the Bookmarks button at the bottom of the screen, and then tap the bookmark name to see it on a map.

The first things you should bookmark are your home and work addresses. These are things you use all the time with Maps, so you might as well bookmark them now to avoid typing them over and over. Also create zip code bookmarks for your home, work, and other locations you frequently visit. Then when you want to find businesses near any of those locations, you can choose the zip code bookmark and type what you're looking for, such as *78729 pizza, 60645 gas station,* or *90201 Starbucks.*

To manage your bookmarks, first tap the Edit button in the top-left corner of the Bookmarks screen. Then:

- **To move a bookmark up or down in the Bookmarks list:** Drag the little icon with three gray bars that appears to the right of the bookmark upward to move the bookmark higher in the list or downward to move the bookmark lower in the list.

- **To delete a bookmark from the Bookmarks list:** Tap the – button to the left of the bookmark's name.

When you're finished using bookmarks, tap the Done button in the top-left corner of the Bookmarks screen to return to the map.

Recents

Maps automatically remembers every location you've searched for in its Recents list (unless you've cleared it, as described next). To see this list, tap the bookmarks icon in the search field and then tap the Recents button at the bottom of the screen. To see a map of a recent item, tap the item's name.

To clear the Recents list, tap the Clear button in the top-left corner of the screen, and then tap the Clear All Recents button.

When you're finished using the Recents list, tap the Done button in the top-right corner of the screen to return to the map.

Contacts

To see a map of a contact's location, tap the bookmarks icon in the search field, and then tap the Contacts button at the bottom of the screen. To see a map of a contact's location, tap the contact's name in the list.

To limit the Contacts list to specific groups (assuming you have some groups in your Contacts list), tap the Groups button in the top-left corner of the screen and then tap the name of the group. Now only contacts in this group are displayed in the list.

When you're finished using the Contacts list, tap the Done button in the top-right corner of the screen to return to the map.

Smart map tricks

The Maps app has more tricks up its sleeve. This section lists a few nifty features you may find useful.

Get route maps and driving directions

You can get route maps and spoken driving directions to any location from any other location in a couple of ways:

- ✓ **If a pushpin is already on the screen:** Tap the pushpin and then tap the little > in a blue circle to the right of the name or description. This action displays the item's Info screen. Now tap the Directions to Here or Directions from Here button to get directions to or from that location, respectively.

- ✓ **When you're looking at a map screen:** Tap the Directions button at the top-left corner of the screen. The Start and End fields appear at the top of the screen. Type the start and end points or select them from your bookmarks, recent maps, or contacts if you prefer. If you want to swap the starting and ending locations, tap the little swirly arrow button to the left of the Start and End fields.

  When the start and end locations are correct, tap the Route button in the top-right corner of the screen and the route map appears.

  If you need to change the start or end location, tap the Clear button in the top-left corner and tap the Directions button again.

  Maps often suggest several routes. The number of suggestions appears at the top of the screen, and the routes appear on the map in blue with cartoon balloons denoting the route number. Tap the blue line or cartoon balloon to select a route, as in Figure 8-7, where Route 2 is selected.

Weird but true: If you type the end location, you have to tap the Route button before you can perform the next step. But if you select the end location from your Bookmarks, Contacts, or Recents list, you won't have to tap the Route button before you perform the next step.

Route 2

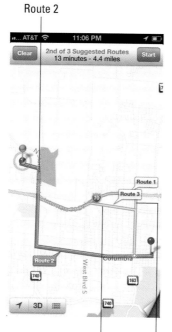

Route 3   Route 1

Figure 8-7: Maps often gives you multiple routes to choose from.

Tap the show traffic button, as described later in this section, to help you decide which route will be most expedient.

The next step is to tap the Start button in the top-right corner to receive spoken turn-by-turn driving directions, as shown in Figure 8-8.

If you prefer your driving directions displayed as a list with all the steps, as shown in Figure 8-9, tap the Maps screen once to display the controls, then tap the List button at the lower left corner.

When you're finished with the step-by-step directions, tap the End button at the top-left corner of the screen to return to the regular map screen and single search field.

We advise plugging the iPhone into a power outlet if at all possible while driving because your phone's GPS hardware can quickly drain the battery.

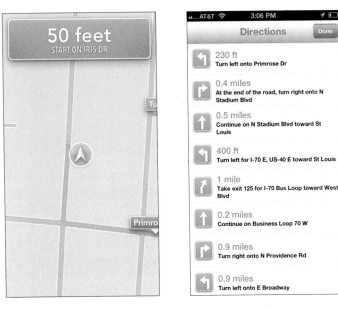

Figure 8-8: The first step in the step-by-step driving directions for the route.

Figure 8-9: Step-by-step driving directions displayed as a list.

Get public transportation information and walking directions

After you've tapped the Directions button, the starting and ending locations screen that appears has three icons near the top: a car, a bus, and a person walking. In the preceding example, we showed directions by car, which is the default.

For public transportation information, tap the bus icon instead. When you do, your iPhone displays a list of the Routing apps available from the App Store (as shown in Figure 8-10). Tap the Routing app you want to download. Figure 8-11 shows a screen from the HopStop Transit Directions app.

For step-by-step directions for walking, tap the person walking icon. Walking directions generally look a lot like driving directions except for your travel time. For example, driving time in Figure 8-7 is approximately 13 minutes with traffic; walking time (not shown) is estimated at 1 hour and 24 minutes.

Figure 8-10: Selecting a Routing app.

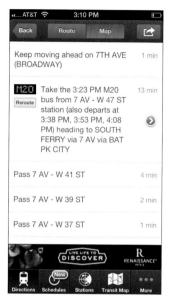

Figure 8-11: Using HopStop Transit Directions.

Get traffic info in real time

You can find out the traffic conditions for whatever map you're viewing by tapping the curling page icon in the lower-right corner and then tapping the Show Traffic button. When you do this, major roadways are color-coded to inform you of the current traffic speed, as shown in Figure 8-12. Here's the key:

- ✔ **Green:** 50 or more miles per hour

- ✔ **Yellow:** 25 to 50 miles per hour

- ✔ **Red:** Under 25 miles per hour

- ✔ **Gray:** No data available at this time

Traffic info isn't available in every location, but the only way to find out is to give it a try. If no color codes appear, assume that traffic information doesn't work for that particular location.

Figure 8-12: Traffic may be moving really slowly (red), kind of slowly (yellow), or nice and fast (green).

More about the Info screen

If a location has a little > in a blue circle to the right of its name or description (refer to Figure 8-2) you can tap the > to see the location's Info screen.

As we explain earlier in this chapter, you can get directions to or from that location, add the location to your bookmarks or contacts, or create a new contact from it. But you can do four more things with a location from its Info screen:

- Tap the phone number to call it.

- Tap the More Info on Yelp to display additional information and reviews from the Yelp website.

- Tap the e-mail address to launch the Mail app and send an e-mail to it (if available).

- Tap the URL to launch Safari and view its website (if available).

Contemplating the Compass

The Compass app, available only on the iPhone 3GS, iPhone 4/4S, and iPhone 5, works like a magnetic needle compass. Launch the Compass app by tapping its icon in the Utilities folder on the second screen, and it shows you the direction you're facing, as shown in Figure 8-13.

But wait — there's more. If you were to tap the little arrowhead icon in the lower-left corner of the Compass screen, the Maps app launches. Now for the cool part: Tap the little arrowhead icon in the lower-left corner of the Maps app two times, and the blue marker grows a little white cone that indicates the direction you're facing, as shown in Figure 8-14.

 Also note that when the map is in compass mode, the little arrowhead icon in its lower-left corner grows a little red cone as well, letting you know that you're now using the compass mode.

Figure 8-13: The Compass app says I'm facing north.

Figure 8-14: The map with the cone says I'm facing north, too.

If you rotate to face a different direction while Maps is in compass mode, the map rotates in real time. So the map always displays the direction you're currently facing, even if you've moved around a bit, which is pretty darn cool.

Taking Stock with Stocks

Stocks is another Internet-enabled app on your iPhone. It's kind of a one-trick pony, but if you need its trick — information about specific stocks — it's a winner.

Every time you open the Stocks app by tapping its icon on the second screen, it displays the latest price for your stocks, with two provisos:

- ✓ The quotes may be delayed by up to 20 minutes.
- ✓ The quotes are updated only if your iPhone can connect to the Internet via either Wi-Fi or a wireless data network.

If your iPhone is running iOS 5 or iOS 6, you can also display the animated Stocks notification by swiping down with one finger from the top of your iPhone's screen.

The first time you open Stocks, you see information for a group of default stocks, funds, and indexes. There are more of them than you can see on the screen at once, so flick upward to scroll down.

Adding and deleting stocks, funds, and indexes

Because the chance of you owning that exact group of stocks, funds, and indexes displayed on the screen is slim, this section shows you how to add your own stocks, funds, or indexes and delete any or all default ones if you want.

Here's how to add a stock, a fund, or an index:

1. **Tap the *i* button in the bottom-right corner of the initial Stocks screen.**

   The *i* is for *info*.

2. **Tap the + button in the top-left corner of the Stocks screen.**

3. **Type the stock symbol or the name of the company, index, or fund.**

4. **Tap the Search button.**

   Stocks finds the company or companies that match your search request.

5. **Tap the one you want to add.**

6. **Repeat Steps 4 and 5 until you're through adding stocks, funds, and indexes.**

7. **Tap the Done button in the top-right corner.**

And here's how to delete a stock (the steps for deleting a fund or an index are the same):

1. **Tap the *i* button in the bottom-right corner of the initial Stocks screen.**

2. **Tap the – button to the left of the stock's name.**

3. **Tap the Delete button that appears to the right of the stock's name.**

4. **Repeat Steps 2 and 3 until all unwanted stocks have been deleted.**

5. **Tap the Done button.**

That's all there is to adding and deleting stocks.

To change the order of the list, tap the *i* button and then drag the three horizontal lines to the right of the stock, fund, or index up or down to its new place in the list.

Details, details, details

To see the details for an item, tap its name to select it, and the lower portion of the screen offers additional information. Note the three small dots under the words *Quotes delayed by 20 minutes*. These dots tell you that there are three screens of information, all shown in Figure 8-15. To switch between these three screens, simply swipe to the left or the right on the lower part of the screen.

To look up additional information about a stock at Yahoo. com, first tap the stock's name to select it and then tap the Y! button in the lower-left corner of the screen. Safari launches and displays the Yahoo.com finance page for that stock.

Yahoo.com button   Three little dots   Info button

Figure 8-15: The Stocks screens.

Weather Watching

Weather is a simple app that provides you with the current weather forecast for the city or cities of your choice. By default, you see a six-day forecast for the chosen city. If the background for the forecast is blue, it's daytime (between 6:00 a.m. and 6:00 p.m.) in that city; if it's a deep purple (as in Figure 8-16), it's nighttime (between 6:00 p.m. and 6:00 a.m.).

If your iPhone is running iOS 5 or iOS 6, you can also display the local weather notification by swiping down with one finger from the top of your iPhone's screen.

To add a city, first tap the *i* button in the bottom-right corner. Next, tap the + button in the upper-left corner, type a city and state or zip code, and tap the Search button in the bottom-right corner of the screen. Finally, tap the name of the found city. Add as many cities as you want this way.

Figure 8-16: The six-day forecast for Austin, Texas.

To delete a city, tap the *i* button in the bottom-right corner. Tap the red – button to the left of its name, and then tap the Delete button that appears to the right of its name.

You can also choose between Fahrenheit and Celsius by first tapping the *i* button in the bottom-right corner and then tapping either the °F or °C button near the bottom of the screen. When you're finished, tap the Done button in the top-right corner of the screen.

If you've added more than one city to Weather, you can switch between them by flicking your finger across the screen to the left or the right.

See the little dots — five gray and one white — at the bottom of the screen in Figure 8-16? They denote the number of cities you have stored (which is six in this case).

The hourly display for each city appears as a scrolling row under the location name, providing the conditions for each hour.

Last, but not least, to see detailed weather information about a city at Yahoo.com, tap the Y! button in the lower-left corner of the screen. Safari launches and then displays the Yahoo.com weather page for the current city.

9

Getting to Know iPhone Apps

In This Chapter

▶ Browsing for cool apps

▶ Getting applications onto your iPhone

A t this writing, more than 700,000 iPhone applications (*apps*) are available for downloading. Some are *third-party* (which means they don't come from Apple); some are free, others cost money; some are useful, others are lame; some are perfectly well behaved, others quit unexpectedly (or worse).

You can obtain and install these applications directly to your iPhone or computer. In this chapter, we show you how to download them to your iPhone.

To use the App Store on your iPhone, it must be connected to the Internet. Before you can use the App Store on your iPhone, however, you first need an Apple ID. If you don't already have one, we suggest you launch iTunes on your computer and click Sign In near the upper-right corner of the iTunes window. Then click Create New Account and follow the on-screen instructions. Or, create your new account directly on your iPhone by following these steps:

1. **Tap the Settings icon on the Home screen.**

2. **Tap iTunes & App Stores in the list of settings.**

3. **Tap Create New Account.**

4. **Follow the on-screen instructions.**

After the App Store knows who you are (and more importantly, knows your credit card number), tap the App Store icon on your Home screen and shop until you drop.

Finding Apps with Your iPhone

Using your iPhone to find apps is pretty darn easy. The only requirement is that you have an Internet connection of some sort — Wi-Fi or wireless data network — to browse, search, download, and install apps.

To get started, tap the App Store icon on your iPhone's Home screen. When you launch the App Store, you see five icons at the bottom of the screen, representing five ways to interact with the store, as shown in Figure 9-1.

Figure 9-1: The icons across the bottom make it easy to browse the App Store.

The first two icons at the bottom of the screen — Featured and Charts — and the Categories button at the top left of the App Store screen offer three ways to browse the virtual shelves of the App Store.

Browsing the iPhone App Store

The Featured section includes several rows of apps — each row is a group of apps with a common theme, like New and Noteworthy or Great Games. Tap any of these app icons to display the details on that app. Flick to the left across a row to display more icons in that group, or throw caution utterly to the wind and tap the See All link above that row (which displays the apps in that group in a full-screen display).

Tap the Genius icon, and the App Store suggests apps you might enjoy based on the apps currently installed on your iPhone.

The Categories screen works a little differently; its main page contains no apps. Instead, it offers a list of categories such as Games, Entertainment, Utilities, Music, and Social Networking, to name a few. Tap a category to see a page with rows displaying apps of that type. Each category's page has several rows, like New, What's Hot, Paid, and Free — to make your browsing easier.

The Charts section works much the same as the Featured section. Its three rows — Paid, Free, and Top Grossing — represent pages of the most popular apps that either cost money (paid and top grossing) or don't (free).

Each row displays a huge number of apps, but you see only three or four at a time on the screen. So remember to flick to the left if you want to see the others.

If you know exactly what you're looking for, instead of simply browsing you can tap the Search icon at the bottom of the App Store screen and type a word or phrase. The following sections show you how to find out more about a particular application.

Checking out the detail screen

To learn more about any application on any page, tap it, and a detail screen like the one shown in Figure 9-2 appears.

Remember that the application description on this screen was written by the developer and may be somewhat biased.

Figure 9-2: This is the detail screen for Remote, a free application from Apple that lets you control iTunes or AppleTV from your iPhone.

Reading reviews from your iPhone

At the top of the detail screen, you find a star rating for that application. Tap the Reviews tab to see a page full of them. At the bottom of that page is another link called More Reviews. Tap it to see (what else?) more reviews.

Downloading an App

To download an application to your iPhone, tap the price button near the top-right corner of its detail screen. In Figure 9-2, it's the rectangle that says *Free*. You may or may not be asked to type your Apple ID password before the App Store disappears and the next iPhone screen with an available spot — where the new application's icon will reside — takes its place. The new icon is slightly dimmed, with the word *Loading* or *Installing* beneath it and a blue progress indicator near its bottom.

By the way, if the app happens to be rated 17+, you see a warning screen after you type your password. You have to click the OK button to confirm that you're over 17 before the app downloads.

The app is now on your iPhone, but it isn't copied to your iTunes library on your Mac or PC until your next sync — unless, of course, you've turned on Automatic Downloads as described earlier in the chapter. If your iPhone suddenly loses its memory (unlikely) or you delete the app from your iPhone before you sync (as described later in this chapter), that app is gone forever. That's the bad news.

The good news is that after you've paid for an app, you can download it again if you need to — from iTunes on your computer or the Updates section of the App Store on your iPhone — and you don't have to pay for it again.

After you download an app to your iPhone, the app is transferred to your iTunes Apps library on your computer the next time you sync your phone. Or you can turn on Automatic Downloads in iTunes on your computer, which is in iTunes Preferences on its Store pane, and the app appears automatically in your computer's iTunes library almost immediately after you purchase the app on your iPhone.

Deleting an App

That's almost everything you need to know about installing apps on your iPhone. However, you might find it helpful to know how to delete an app.

You can delete an app in two ways: in iTunes on your computer or directly from your iPhone.

To delete an app in iTunes, click Apps in the source list and then do one of the following:

- ↙ Click the app's icon to select it and then choose Edit↪Delete.
- ↙ Right-click the app's icon and choose Delete.

Either way, you see a dialog box asking whether you're sure you want to remove the selected app. If you click the Remove button, the app is removed from your computer's iTunes library, as well as from any iPhone that syncs with your iTunes library.

You can't delete any Apple apps that came with your iPhone, but here's how to delete other apps you've downloaded on your iPhone:

1. **Press and hold any icon until all the icons begin to jiggle.**

2. **Tap the little x in the upper-left corner of the app you want to delete.**

   A dialog box appears, informing you that deleting this app also deletes all its data.

3. **Tap the Delete button.**

Deleting an app from your iPhone this way doesn't get rid of it permanently. It remains in your iTunes library on your computer until you delete it from iTunes. Put another way: Even though you deleted the app from your iPhone, it's still in your iTunes library. If you want to get rid of an app for good and for always after you delete it on your iPhone, you also must delete it from your iTunes library. Even then it's not *really* gone forever because you can download purchased apps again for free.

10

When Good iPhones Go Bad

In This Chapter

▶ Fixing iPhone issues

▶ Dealing with network and calling problems

▶ Eliminating that sinking feeling when you can't sync

▶ Perusing the Apple website and discussion forums

▶ Sending your iPhone to an Apple Store

*I*n our experience, iPhones are usually reliable devices. And, most users we talk to report trouble-free operation. Notice our use of the word *most*. That's because every so often, a good iPhone goes bad. It's not a common occurrence, but it does happen. So in this chapter, we look at the types of bad things that can happen, along with suggestions for fixing them.

What kind of bad things are we talking about? Well, we're referring to problems involving

▮ ✔ The phone itself

▮ ✔ Making or receiving calls

▮ ✔ Wireless networks

▮ ✔ Syncing, computers (both Mac and PC) or iTunes

After all the troubleshooting, we tell you how to get even more help if nothing we suggest does the trick.

iPhone Issues

Our first category of troubleshooting techniques applies to an iPhone that's frozen or otherwise acting up. The recommended procedure when this happens is to perform the six *Rs* in sequence:

- Recharge
- Restart
- Reset your iPhone
- Remove your content
- Reset settings and content
- Restore

If your iPhone acts up on you — if it freezes, doesn't wake up from sleep, doesn't do something it used to do, or in any other way acts improperly — don't panic; this section describes the things you should try, in the order that we (and Apple) recommend.

If the first technique doesn't do the trick, go on to the second. If the second one doesn't work, try the third. And so on.

Recharge

If your iPhone acts up in any way, shape, or form, the first thing you should try is to give its battery a full recharge.

Don't plug the iPhone's Lightning connector–to–USB cable into a USB port on your keyboard, monitor, or USB hub. You need to plug the cable into one of the USB ports on your computer itself, because the USB ports on your computer supply more power than the other ports.

Note that you can use the included USB power adapter to recharge your iPhone from an AC outlet rather than from a computer (which takes significantly less time). So if your iPhone isn't charging when you connect it to your computer, try charging it from a wall outlet instead.

Restart

If you recharge your iPhone and it still misbehaves, the next thing to try is restarting it. Just as restarting a computer often fixes problems, restarting your iPhone sometimes works wonders.

Here's how to restart:

1. **Press and hold the sleep/wake button.**

2. **Slide the red slider to turn off the iPhone, and then wait a few seconds.**

3. **Press and hold the sleep/wake button again until the Apple logo appears on the screen.**

4. **If your phone is still frozen, misbehaves, or doesn't start, do a force-quit as follows, and then try Steps 1–3 again.**

   - If you have a first-generation iPhone or iPhone 3G, force-quit by pressing and holding the Home button for 6 to 10 seconds.

   - If you have an iPhone 3GS, 4/4S, or 5, force-quit as follows: Press and hold the sleep/wake button until the red Slide to Power Off button appears and then release the sleep/wake button. Don't drag the red slider. Instead, with the red slider still on the screen, press and hold the Home button for 6 to 15 seconds.

If these steps don't get your iPhone back up and running, move on to the third *R,* resetting your iPhone.

Reset your iPhone

To reset your iPhone, merely press and hold the sleep/wake button while pressing and holding the Home button on the front. When you see the Apple logo, you can release both buttons.

Resetting your iPhone is like forcing your computer to restart after a crash. Your data shouldn't be affected by a reset. So don't be shy about giving this technique a try. In many cases, your iPhone goes back to normal after you reset it this way.

Remember to press *and hold* both the sleep/wake button and the Home button. If you press both and then release them, you create a *screen shot* — a picture of whatever is on your screen at the time — rather than reset your iPhone. (This type of screen picture, by the way, is stored in the Photos app's Camera Roll. Find out more about this feature at the end of Chapter 11.)

Unfortunately, sometimes resetting *doesn't* do the trick. When that's the case, you have to take stronger measures.

Remove content

If you've been reading along in this chapter, nothing you've done should have taken more than a minute or two. We hate to tell you, but that's about to change because the next thing you should try is removing some or all of your data, to see whether it's the cause of your troubles.

To do so, you need to sync your iPhone and reconfigure it so that some or all of your files are removed from the phone. The problem could be within your iCloud data (contacts, calendar data. bookmarks, or notes), or there may be a problem within your digital media (songs, photos, videos, audiobooks, or podcasts). If you suspect a particular data type — for example, you suspect your photos because whenever you tap the Photos icon on the Home screen, your iPhone freezes — try removing that type of data first.

Or, if you have no suspicions, deselect every item on every tab in iTunes (Info, Apps, Music, Movies, Photos, and so on) and then sync. When you're finished, your iPhone should have no data on it.

If that method fixed the problem, try restoring your data, one type at a time. If the problem returns, you have to keep experimenting to determine which particular data type or file is causing the problem.

If you're still having problems, the next step is to reset your iPhone's settings.

Reset settings and content

Resetting involves two steps: The first one, resetting your iPhone settings, resets every iPhone *setting* to its default — the way it was when you took it out of the box. It's important to note that resetting the iPhone's settings does *not* erase any of your data or media. The only downside is that you may have to go back and change some settings afterward (for example, the amount of time your iPhone waits before turning off the display), so you can try this step without trepidation. Tap the Settings icon on your Home screen, tap General, tap Reset, and then tap Reset All Settings.

 Be careful *not* to tap Erase All Content and Settings, at least not yet. Erasing all content takes more time to recover from (because your next sync takes a long time), so try Reset All Settings first.

At this point, you could try resetting some of the other options available on the Reset screen, such as Reset Network Settings, Reset Keyboard Dictionary, Reset Home Screen Layout, or Reset Location Warnings. It's not likely to help but might be worth a try before you resort to erasing all content and settings, as we're about to describe. (Note that resetting your Home screen layout resets the order of *all* apps on your iPhone — including apps that you've added to folders.)

Now, if resetting all settings didn't cure your iPhone, you have to try Erase All Content and Settings. (Read the next Warning first.) You find that option in the same place as Reset All Settings (tap Settings, General, and Reset).

 This strategy deletes *everything* from your iPhone — all your data, media, and settings. Because all these items are either stored on your computer or iCloud — at least in theory — you should be able to put things back the way they were during your next sync. But you lose any photos you've taken, as well as contacts, calendar events, and any playlists you've created or modified since your last sync.

After using Erase All Content and Settings, check to see whether your iPhone works properly. If it doesn't cure what ails your iPhone, the final *R,* restoring your iPhone using iTunes, can help.

Restore

Before you give up the ghost on your poor, sick iPhone, you can try one more thing. Connect your iPhone to your computer as though you were about to sync. But when the iPhone appears in the iTunes source list, click the Restore button on the Summary tab. This action erases all your data and media and resets all your settings.

 Because all your data and media still exist on your computer or within iCloud (except for photos you've taken, contacts, calendar events, Passbook items, notes, and playlists you've created or modified since your last sync, or iTunes or App Store content you've purchased or downloaded since your last sync, as noted previously), you shouldn't lose anything by restoring. Your next sync will take longer than usual, and you may have to reset settings you've changed since you got your iPhone. But other than those inconveniences, restoring shouldn't cause you any trouble. Remember, you can always re-download content you've purchased from the iTunes Store.

If you've tried every trick in the book and still have a malfunctioning iPhone, it's time to consider shipping it off to the iPhone hospital (better known as Apple, Inc.). The repair is free if your iPhone is still under its one-year limited warranty. Although you may be able to get your iPhone serviced by your provider or by mail, we recommend that you take it to your nearest Apple Store: No one knows your iPhone like Apple. One of the geniuses at the Apple Store may be able to fix whatever is wrong without sending your iPhone away for repairs.

Problems with Calling or Networks

If you're having problems making or receiving calls, problems sending or receiving SMS text messages or iMessages, or problems with Wi-Fi or your wireless carrier's data network, this section may help. The techniques here are short and sweet — except for the last one, restore. Restore, which we describe in the preceding section, is still inconvenient and time consuming, and it still entails erasing all your data and media and then restoring it.

First, here are some simple steps that may help. Once again, we suggest that you try them in this order (and so does Apple):

1. **Check the cell signal icon in the upper-left corner of the screen.**

   If you don't have at least one or two bars, you may not be able to use the phone or messaging function.

2. **Make sure you haven't left your iPhone in airplane mode.**

   In airplane mode, all network-dependent features are disabled, so you can't make or receive phone calls, send or receive messages, or use any apps or features that require a Wi-Fi or data network connection (that is, Mail, Safari, Siri, Stocks, Maps, and Weather). You can always tell when you're in airplane mode because your iPhone displays the tiny airplane icon at the top left of the screen.

3. **Try moving around.**

   Changing your location by as little as a few feet can sometimes mean the difference between four bars and zero bars or being able to use a Wi-Fi or wireless data network or not. If you're inside, try going outside. If you're outside, try moving 10 or 20 paces in any direction. Keep an eye on the cell signal or Wi-Fi icon as you move around, and stop when you see more bars than you saw before.

4. **Try changing your grip on the phone (or if it's an iPhone 4/4S or 5, try using a case).**

   Apple says, "Gripping any mobile phone will result in some attenuation of its antenna performance, with certain places being worse than others depending on the placement of the antennas. This is a fact of life for every wireless phone. If you ever experience this on your iPhone 4 or 4S, avoid gripping it in the lower-left corner in a way that covers both sides of the black strip in the metal band, or simply use one of many available cases."

5. **Turn on airplane mode by tapping Settings on the Home screen and then tapping the airplane mode On/Off switch to turn it on. Wait 15 or 20 seconds and then turn it off again.**

Toggling airplane mode on and off like this resets both the Wi-Fi and wireless data-network connections. If your network connection was the problem, toggling airplane mode on and off may correct it.

6. Restart your iPhone.

If you've forgotten how, refer to the "Restart" section, a few pages back. Restarting your iPhone is often all it takes to fix whatever was wrong.

7. Make sure your SIM card is firmly seated.

A *SIM* (Subscriber Identity Module) card is a removable smart card used to identify mobile phones. Users can change phones by moving the SIM card from one phone to another.

To remove the SIM card, use the included SIM-eject tool (if you have an iPhone 3G or 3GS), or find a fine-gauge paper clip and straighten one end, and then stick the straight end *gently* into the hole on the SIM tray, as shown in Figure 10-1 for the iPhone 3G and 3GS and Figure 10-2 for the iPhone 4/4S and 5.

When the SIM tray slides out, carefully lift out the SIM card and then reinsert it, making sure it's firmly situated in the tray before you *gently* push the tray back in until it locks.

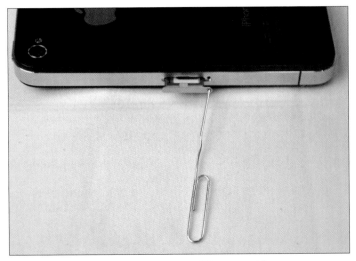

Figure 10-1: Removing the SIM tray on an iPhone 4 or 4S.

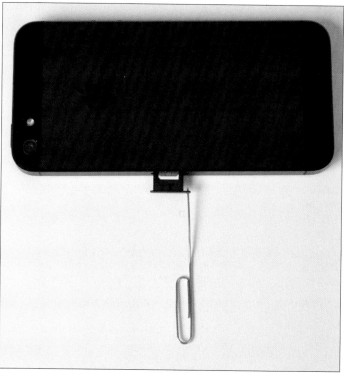

Figure 10-2: Removing the SIM tray on an iPhone 5.

If none of the preceding suggestions fixes your network issues, try restoring your iPhone as described previously in the "Restore" section.

Performing a restore deletes everything on your iPhone — all your data, media, and settings. You should be able to put things back the way they were with your next sync. If that doesn't happen, for whatever reason, you can't say we didn't warn you.

Sync, Computer, or iTunes Issues

The last category of troubleshooting techniques in this chapter applies to issues that involve USB synchronization and computer-iPhone relations. If you're having problems syncing or your computer doesn't recognize your iPhone when you connect it, here are some things to try.

Once again, we suggest that you try these procedures in the order they're presented here:

1. **Recharge your iPhone.**

   If you didn't try it previously, try it now. Go back to the "iPhone Issues" section, at the beginning of this chapter, and read what we say about recharging your iPhone. Every word there applies here.

2. **Try a different USB port or a different cable if you have one available.**

   It doesn't happen often, but occasionally USB ports and cables go bad. When they do, they invariably cause sync and connection problems. Always make sure that a bad USB port or cable isn't to blame.

   If you don't remember what we said about using USB ports on your computer rather than the ones on your keyboard, monitor, or hub, we suggest that you reread the "Recharge" section, earlier in this chapter.

    Unfortunately, the Lightning connector that Apple has introduced for the iPhone 5 does not work directly with the older USB-to-30 pin cable used with iPods, iPhones and iPads for many years. However, there is an adapter available that converts the Lightning connector to the 30-pin dock connector, so if you happen to have one of those cables and the adapter handy, give it a try.

3. **Restart your iPhone and try to sync again.**

   We describe restarting in full and loving detail in the "Restart" section, earlier in this chapter.

4. **Restart your computer.**

   We have found that restarting your computer often fixes issues with syncing your iPhone.

    Restarting your computer can fix non-iPhone issues as well. It's a good idea to reboot your computer before you do any kind of troubleshooting.

5. Reinstall iTunes.

Even if you have an iTunes installer handy, you probably should visit the Apple website and download the latest-and-greatest version, just in case. You'll always find the latest version of iTunes at `www.apple.com/itunes/download` (we used version 10.7 with this book).

More Help on Apple.com

If you try everything we suggest earlier in this chapter and still have problems, don't give up just yet. This section describes a few places you may find helpful. We recommend that you check out some or all of them before you throw in the towel and smash your iPhone into tiny little pieces (or ship it back to Apple for repairs, as described in the next section).

First, Apple offers an excellent set of support resources on its website at `www.apple.com/support/iphone`. You can browse support issues by category, search for a problem by keyword, or even get personalized help by phone, as shown in Figure 10-3.

Discussion communities

Browse by category   Search by keyword

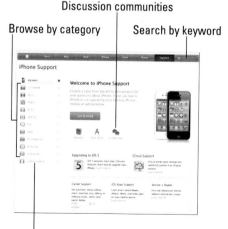

Get personalized help

Figure 10-3: The Apple iPhone support pages offer several kinds of helpful information.

While you're visiting the Apple support pages, another section could be helpful: the discussion forums. You find them at http://discussions.apple.com, and they're chock-full of questions and answers from other iPhone users. Our experience has been that if you can't find an answer to a support question elsewhere, you can often find something helpful in these forums. You can browse by category, such as "Integrating iPhone into Your Digital Life" (part of the "Using iPhone" category), as shown in Figure 10-4, or search by keyword.

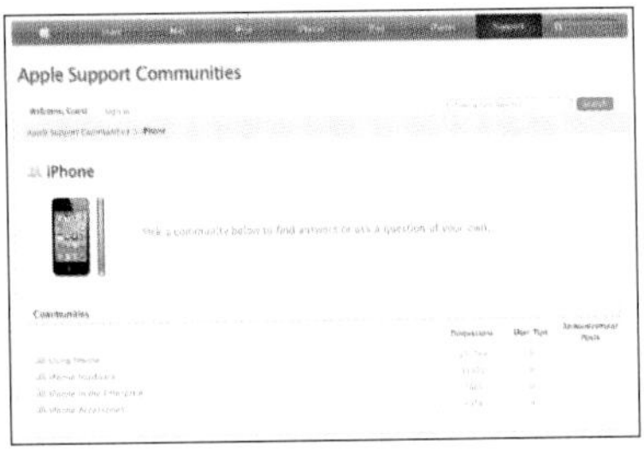

Figure 10-4: Four iPhone communities have thousands of discussions about all things iPhone.

Either way, you find thousands of discussions about almost every aspect of using your iPhone. Better still, frequently you can find the answer to your question or a helpful suggestion.

Now for the best part: If you can't find a solution by browsing or searching, you can post your question in the appropriate Apple discussion forum. Check back in a few days (or even in a few hours), and some helpful iPhone user may well have replied with the answer. If you've never tried this fabulous tool, you're missing out on one of the greatest support resources available anywhere.

Last, but certainly not least, before you give up the ghost, you might want to try a carefully worded Google search. It couldn't hurt, and you might just find the solution you spent hours searching for.

11

Ten (Or So) iPhone Tips

*A*fter spending quality time with our iPhones, we've discovered lots of helpful hints, tips, and shortcuts. In this chapter, we share some of our faves.

Do the Slide

What we call the *slide* can help you type more accurately and type punctuation and numerals faster than ever before.

You start by performing the first half of a tap. That is, you touch your finger to the screen but don't lift it up. Without lifting your finger, slide it onto the key you want to type. You'll know you're on the right key because it pop ups — enlarges.

Try the slide during normal typing. Stab at a key; if you miss, rather than lifting your finger, backspacing, and trying again, do the slide onto the proper key. After you get the hang of it, you'll see that it saves time and improves your accuracy.

The next time you need to type a punctuation mark or number, try this technique:

1. **Start a slide action with your finger on the *123* key (the key to the left of the Space key when the alphabetical keyboard is active) — don't lift your finger yet.**

2. **When the punctuation and numeric keyboard appears on-screen, slide your finger onto the punctuation mark or number you want to type.**

3. **Lift your finger.**

The punctuation and numeric keyboard disappears and the alphabetical keyboard reappears — all without tapping the *123* key to display the punctuation and numeric keyboard and without tapping the *ABC* key.

Use Auto Apostrophes

The auto-correction software on the iPhone is your friend. You can type *dont* to get to *don't,* and *cant* to get to *can't.* One exception: the iPhone can't distinguish between *it's,* the contraction of "it is," and *its,* the possessive adjective and possessive pronoun.

Make Rejection Work for You

If the auto-correct suggestion isn't the word you want, instead of ignoring it, reject it. Finish typing the word and then tap the *x* to reject the suggestion before you type another word. Doing so makes your iPhone more likely to accept your word the next time you type it and less likely to make the same incorrect suggestion again.

View the iPhone's Capacity

When your iPhone is selected in the source list in iTunes, you see a colorful chart at the bottom of the screen that tells you how your iPhone's capacity is being used by your media and other data. By default, the chart shows the amount of space your audio, video, and photo files use on your iPhone in megabytes (MB) or gigabytes (GB). When you click any of the file headings beneath the colorful chart, it cycles through two more slightly different displays. The first click changes the display from the amount of space used to the number of items (audio, video, and photos) you have stored. Click once more, and the display changes to the total playing time for audio and video. Before leaving on a trip, it can be helpful to know that you have 5.6 hours of video and 1.8 days of audio.

URL and Phone Number Tricks

The iPhone does something special when it encounters a phone number or URL in an e-mail or message. The iPhone interprets as a phone number any sequence of numbers that looks like a phone number: 1-123-555-4567, 555-4567, 1.123.555.4567, and so on. The same goes for sequences of characters that look like a web address, such as `http://www.WebSiteName.com` or `www.WebSiteName.com`. When the iPhone sees what it assumes to be a URL, it appears as a blue link on your screen.

If you tap a phone number or URL sequence like the ones just shown, the iPhone does the right thing. It launches the Phone application and dials the number or launches Safari and takes you to the appropriate web page for a URL.

What's even more useful is the way Safari handles phone numbers and URLs. When you encounter a phone number on a web page, give it a tap. A little dialog box appears on the screen displaying that phone number and offering you a choice of two buttons: Call or Cancel. Tap Call to switch to the Phone application and dial the number; tap Cancel to return to the web page.

Here's a cool Safari trick with links. If you press and hold on a link rather than tapping it, a little floating text bubble appears and shows you the underlying URL.

Finally, here's one last Safari trick. If you press and hold on most graphic images, a Save Image button appears. Tap it and the picture is saved to the Camera Roll in the Photos application.

Share the Love

Ever stumble on a web page you just have to share with a buddy? The iPhone makes it dead simple, using a veritable host of options! From the site in question, tap the action button at the bottom of the browser (which looks like a square sprouting a curved arrow).

Your first sharing option is a Mail message. Tap the Mail button and a mail message appears with the subject line pre-populated with the name of the website you're visiting, and the body of the message pre-populated with the URL. Just type something in the message body (or don't), supply your pal's e-mail address, and tap the Send button.

The Action button also sports buttons for Twitter and Facebook — tap either button and you can immediately begin typing the body of your Twitter tweet or Facebook post. Again, the URL is included automatically.

Finally, tap Message to create a new text message with the URL, ready for you to address.

Choose a Safari Home Page

You may have noticed that there's no home page website on the iPhone version of Safari as there is in the Mac and PC versions of the browser. Instead, when you tap the Safari icon, you return to the last site you visited. You can create an icon for the page you want to use as your home page by creating a *web clip* of a web page. Here's how to do it:

1. **Open the web page you want to use as your home page and tap the action button.**

2. **Tap the Add to Home Screen button.**

   An icon to open this page appears on the next screen with an available spot.

3. **Tap this new web clip icon instead of the Safari icon, and Safari opens to your home page instead of to the last page you visited.**

Storing Files

A tiny Massachusetts software company known as Ecamm Network is selling an inexpensive piece of Mac OS X software that lets you copy files from your computer to your iPhone and copy files from the iPhone to a computer. (There is no Windows version.) Better still, you can try the $29.95 program called PhoneView for a week before deciding whether you want to buy it. Go to www.ecamm.com to fetch the free demo.

In a nutshell, here's how it works. After downloading the software onto your Mac, double-click the program's icon to start it. To transfer files and folders to the iPhone (assuming there's room on the device), click the Copy To iPhone button on the toolbar and click to select the files you want to copy. The files are copied into the appropriate folder on the iPhone. Alternatively, you can drag files and folders from the Mac desktop or a folder into the PhoneView browser.

To go the other way and copy files from your iPhone to your computer, highlight the files or folders you want copied and click the Copy From iPhone button on the toolbar. Select the destination on your Mac where you want to store the files and then click Save. You can also drag files and folders from the PhoneView file browser onto the Mac desktop or folder. Or you can double-click a file in the PhoneView browser to download it to your Mac's Documents folder.

Getting Apps out of the Multitasking Tray

The multitasking offered by iOS 5 and iOS 6 is great, but sometimes you don't want to see an app's icon in the multitasking tray. It's easy to remove any app that's cluttering up your tray. Here's how to remove an app icon from the multitasking tray:

1. **Double-press the Home button.**

   The multitasking tray appears.

2. **Press any icon in the tray until all the icons begin to wiggle and display a little red – symbol.**

3. **Tap the little red – symbol for the app (or apps) you want to remove from the tray.**

   The app disappears from the multitasking tray. To fill the gap in the tray, apps slide to the left. (Icons from the group of apps you'd see if you swiped from right to left on the tray slide onto the screen as needed.)

4. **Press the Home button to end the wiggling and hide the red – symbols.**

5. **Press the Home button again to dismiss the multitasking tray.**

You can use this trick to stop an app that's running in the background, too. For example, if Pandora Radio is playing in the background and you decide you've had enough Pandora for now, just follow the preceding steps and Pandora will shut the heck up. Without this trick, you'd have to open Pandora, tap the Pause button, and then press the Home button to close Pandora (but the Pandora icon remains in the multitasking tray).

The bottom line is that using this tip is an easier, faster way to quit an app that's running in the background, as well as the only way (short of restarting your iPhone) to remove an icon from your multitasking tray.

Take a Snapshot of the Screen

Press the Sleep/Wake button at the same time you press the Home button, but just for an instant. The iPhone grabs a snapshot of whatever is on the screen.

The picture lands in the iPhone's Camera Roll, from where you can synchronize it with your PC or Mac, include it in your Photo Stream, or assign it to a Shared Photo Stream. And from there, the possibilities are endless. Why, your picture could wind up just about anywhere, including in a *For Dummies* book.

Assault on batteries

Because this is a chapter of tips and hints, we'd be remiss if we didn't include some ways that you can extend your battery life. First and foremost: If you use a carrying case, charging the iPhone while it's in that case may generate more heat than is healthy. Overheating is bad for both battery capacity and battery life. So take the iPhone out of the case before you charge it.

If you're not using a 3G/4G or Wi-Fi network, or a Bluetooth device (such as a headset or car kit), consider turning off the Wi-Fi, Cellular and Bluetooth features you don't need in Settings. Doing so could mean the difference between running out of juice and being able to make that important call later in the day.

Activate Auto-Brightness to enable the screen brightness to adjust based on current lighting conditions, which can be easier on your battery. Tap Settings on the Home screen, tap Brightness & Wallpaper, and then tap the On/Off switch, if necessary, to turn it on.

Turning off Location Services (tap Settings, tap Privacy, tap Location Services, and then tap the On/Off switch) and turning off Push (tap Settings, tap Mail, Contacts, Calendars, tap Fetch New Data, and then tap the On/Off switch) can also help to conserve battery life.

Finally, turning on EQ (see Chapter 5) when you listen to music can make it sound better, but it also uses more processing power. If you've added EQ to tracks in iTunes using the Track Info window, and you want to retain the EQ from iTunes, set the EQ on your iPhone to flat. Because you're not turning off EQ, your battery life will be slightly worse but your

(continued)

(continued)

songs will sound just the way you expect them to sound. Either way, to alter your EQ settings, tap Settings on the Home screen, tap Music, and then tap EQ.

Apple says a properly maintained iPhone battery will retain up to 80 percent of its original capacity after 400 full charge and discharge cycles. You can replace the battery at any time if it no longer holds sufficient charge. Your one-year limited warranty includes the replacement

of a defective battery. Coverage jumps to two years with the AppleCare or AppleCare+ Protection Plans. Apple will replace the battery if it drops below 50 percent of its original capacity.

If your iPhone is out of warranty, Apple will replace the battery for $79 plus $6.95 shipping, plus local tax, and will also dispose of your old battery in an environmentally friendly manner.

The Way-Cool, Semi-Hidden, Audio Scrub Speed Tip

Here's the situation: You're listening to a podcast or audiobook and trying to find the beginning of a specific segment by moving the scrubber left and right. The only problem is that the scrubber isn't very precise and your fat finger keeps moving it too far one way or the other. Never fear — your iPhone has a wonderful (albeit somewhat hidden) fix. Just press your finger on the scrubber (that little round dot on the scrubber bar), but instead of sliding your finger to the left or right, slide it downward toward the bottom of the screen. As you slide, the scrubbing speed changes like magic and the amount of change is displayed above the scrubber bar. The default (normal) speed is called high-speed scrubbing; when you slide your finger downward, the speed changes to half-speed scrubbing, then to quarter-speed scrubbing, and finally to fine scrubbing. This scrub trick is easier to do than to explain, so give it a try.

While you're sliding, keep an eye on the elapsed time and remaining time indicators because they provide useful feedback on the current scrubbing speed.

Index